Naturalogy

Naturalogy

The study of logical natural health.

SPENCER PULLIN

A&F

Alice&Fred Books

A&F
Alice&Fred Books

First published in Great Britain in 2020 by

Alice & Fred Books
Sidney House
34 Station Road
Tiptree
Essex
CO5 0AZ

ISBN: 978-0-9560965-6-2

Book design and typesetting by Ashdown Creative
www.ashdowncreative.co.uk

The contents of this book do not constitute medical advice and should not be used to treat any medical condition. Always refer to your trusted health professional if in doubt.

For my wife Julia, as without you I would be destined
for a shorter, emptier life... and for my mum,
for putting the two of us together.

Acknowledgements

I must thank Dr Vicky Cole for first putting me on to a path of real health and showing me the true nature of what it means to be well. Vicky introduced me to Dr James Chestnut's incredible science, reason and logic, and everything I've discovered since has led on from this.

Bruce Lipton has shown me the incredible power of the mind and that it is nonsense to consider health by only investigating the physical body. He was also the first person to give me the truth about how our genes function instead of the dogma and misunderstanding that the general public are given.

The work of Gabor Maté has only further reinforced my new understanding.

Contents

CHAPTER 1

Good Health is Logical, Easy and Inevitable

I have been compelled to write this book for several years. I'm not originally from a health care background but have been working in that arena now since a drastic career change in 2006. I'm not qualified in any area of health and am just a normal person, probably very similar to you.

I was originally an electrical engineer in the steel industry but had the great fortune to fall in love with, and eventually marry, a chiropractor. Julia was recently qualified when we first met and, after a few years, we both became increasingly aware of what true health is and, more importantly, what it isn't. Health is not merely the absence of any symptoms either with or without drugs. Health is the state of being where every single cell in your body is functioning as it should, with all the raw ingredients it needs and without having to deal with anything it doesn't need or isn't built to process.

So why should you read this book and take any notice of me? Surely your doctor knows best, not some ex-electrician who works in an "alternative health" clinic. If you're convinced that your medical doctor has all the answers, that health can only come from taking the pills he or she prescribes, and that anyone who claims you can enjoy great health and quality of life without ever visiting your doctor is clearly a charlatan, then the content of this book is probably not for you. However, if you've become increasingly confused by the conflicting information about health, what's good or bad for you and how this advice seems to change every year, then perhaps you're ready to challenge the status quo and use some logic to make better choices.

During the past ten years of my life, I've attended hundreds of hours of seminars and read countless books from some truly visionary people, all unpicking the truth about how to be well. These people are well respected in their particular field and have some brilliant research to back up their claims. All this information that I've been exposed to has helped me to formulate what I consider to be a simple set of guidelines, based on logic and common sense, to greatly stack the odds in your favour towards living a long, productive life free from chronic disease.

You don't have to live like a puritan and replace pleasure with hardship in your life, and you'll probably see, as you read on, that many of the things you've been told are bad for you are not at all, and that the things you believe are beneficial do you more harm than good. Indeed, as long as you're following the principles for the majority of the time, you should enjoy great health and a long, happy life as a result. The trick is to not get overwhelmed by the changes required and just allow them to happen gradually and consciously until they become the norm.

Too many times people embark on a radical shift in lifestyle, changing lots of things all at the same time and it becomes stressful and unsustainable. They then return back to where they were before, feeling like a failure and that it's impossible. Gradually bringing in new habits is a bit like drifting down a beautiful river in a boat and taking in the journey as it happens, noticing the changes along the way and enjoying that journey. Making small changes one at a time, adding new, healthy habits gradually as you go, will have a huge, positive impact on preventing you from developing a chronic illness. Incorporating them into your social life wherever you can and making them fun will help them to stick.

I have no particular agenda to push or pills to sell, but just want to demystify health and empower everyone to do the same. The contents of this book are not a plan to turn you into an athlete. They don't involve eating an unusual or extreme diet, but just give you some common sense strategies that I hope you'll see are logical and sensible.

I intend to show you that being thin or having the body of an Adonis does not mean you are healthy. How your body looks can give some clues about your health status but it isn't the whole story. The cemeteries are full of people who died far too young with thin "healthy-looking" bodies, and there are millions of people who have a little more body weight than they think they should do, who live a long life into their eighties, nineties and beyond. Indeed, there are lots of unhealthy ways of losing weight and being thin, and they should be avoided at all costs. Diet foods, crash diets and drugs can all make the number on the scale lower but none of them will lead to a longer, healthier life. Purely focusing on your weight as an indicator of health is dangerous. Making choices with the sole intention of lowering the number on the bathroom scales could be unpleasant and have the opposite effect to the one you'd hoped for. I've changed my target personally and encourage you to do the same. I've stopped aiming for weight loss and instead focus on health gain. Your weight will take care of itself and settle at the correct level for you once your decisions are only aimed at gaining more health.

I'd be very surprised if you didn't already know one thing you could do now that would lead to greater health for you. Repeating this thing regularly for a period of time would then maximise the improvement and, after doing it for a year, would you be more or less healthy?

You'd obviously be healthier than you would have been had you not been doing that one thing. It could be something as simple as eating an apple every day or walking for an hour every Monday lunchtime. Little, positive changes to your lifestyle, consciously added, become habits that you miss when they're not there and their positive benefits are cumulative over time.

Imagine now that over the year you'd added ten positive things, or 20 even. Greater health can be easily gained by gradually adding positive habits and routines into your daily life. Once you become aware of the impact your positive changes are having, you'll naturally want to cut out some of the negative habits you've accumulated over your life. It doesn't all have to start now, immediately. You don't have to wait for the 1st January and declare your New Year's resolution is to change everything about your life overnight, only to last about a week before you find it all too much and go back to how you were on the 31st December, but now also feeling like a failure. Stopping doing the things that bring you pleasure is stressful and often unsustainable. It's no wonder most lifestyle changes don't stick.

It's all about my genes, so why bother?

My dad was diagnosed with bowel cancer at 45. His work life involved a large amount of stress, a lot of late nights and early mornings and not much exercise. He drank quite a lot of alcohol, ate a lot of convenience foods and was overweight. In these respects, he wasn't different from a lot of people. Many of us have sedentary jobs, like a drink and enjoy the ease of pre-packed or ready-made foods. The thought of spending hours in a gym fills us with revulsion. That's for the skinny people in their tight-fitting, athletic clothing. We know we could probably follow a healthier lifestyle but does it really make that much difference anyway? It's all genetic, isn't it? There's a breast cancer gene and a bowel cancer gene. There are genes that cause diabetes and genes that cause heart disease. We hear about them all the time, on the TV and in the newspapers. I've even read about the so-called hangover gene, for goodness' sake! Genetic illnesses – there's little we can do except wait for some symptoms to appear and then go and see the GP, who hopefully won't fob us off on our first visit and will send us for some tests with a specialist. Then we'll get some pills, some surgery or a course of chemotherapy, and live in fear with our fingers crossed, enduring those sympathetic facial expressions from our friends and family.

This is what happened to my dad. He fought bravely for three years, enduring several surgeries, chemotherapy and radiotherapy. He had so many meetings with his oncologist and other specialists where he'd been dreading the appointment but praying for good news, only to see the look on their faces when they had nothing to offer him but the hopelessness of it all. He'd been dealt a bad hand; there was nothing he could do; it wasn't his fault. It's genetic.

This is what the majority of people have been taught to believe: that cancer, diabetes, heart disease, obesity, Alzheimer's and the like are genetic. A genetic illness. It's not your fault. It's your genes. It's bad luck.

That's why the first question you're asked when you arrive at the GP's or the hospital is, "Has anyone in your immediate family been diagnosed with this before?" If the answer is yes, then, "Ah, well, it's genetic, you see." Immediately all hope is lost. If the answer is no, we're still told that it's a genetic illness! How can it be the same cause when the answers are different? It's a completely hopeless situation and we're told we are victims of our genetic makeup.

The problem is, my dad's genes were passed to him by his parents. My granddad, his dad, is still going strong at 95. Now, he's by no means able to run a marathon and has a lot of the aches and pains we'd associate with someone of his age, but he lives in his own home and still looks after himself, shopping, cooking and cleaning etc. Mentally, he's as sharp as he's ever been. He's had a few health challenges in the past 15 years or so but nothing serious, and some of that will be because he's never had any guidance on his lifestyle and how it can affect his health. However, he had a very physical job for most of his working life, has never smoked, is not a drinker and the vast majority of his food was cooked from fresh every day.

Your genes are not your destiny

Unless you have a real genetic condition, such as Down syndrome or cystic fibrosis, the chances are you have an adequate set of genes for great health. Your body is an amazing ecosystem of 50 to 75 trillion cells all working together to create the life that you experience daily. Your genome has evolved over millions of years and through thousands of generations of your ancestors, successively adapting and improving to thrive in the environment that it is to live in.

However, and this is probably the main point of this chapter, your genes are not in control. That's right, your genes are not in control! Your genes have no autonomy or self-determinism. A gene doesn't suddenly decide to switch on or off or grow a tumour in your breast or prostate tissue. Genes are inanimate unless they are brought into use by an outside stimulus. They can only respond to environmental signals. And by environment, I'm not just referring to the air you breathe or the countryside around your home. I mean every aspect of the things your body comes into contact with, from the foods you eat to the products you put on your skin; from the activities you do to the thoughts you have. They all make up the environment that provides the signals that your genes, and hence your body, respond to.

Your genes can be thought of as a huge collection of recipes or instructions, whose individual result is to produce a protein in response to an environmental stimulus. They don't have control. You wouldn't expect to open a cookery book in your kitchen at the page of your favourite meal and for the recipe to create the food for you. Your genetic recipes are exactly the same.

The environment that thousands of your generations of ancestors found themselves in, or produced for themselves by their actions, shaped your current genome. If your ancestors' genes were not suited to the foods they ate, the activity levels they experienced and the thoughts they had, they would likely not have survived long enough to reproduce successfully. The numbers of other similar early humans with the same genetic traits would also have struggled to thrive, so their numbers would have dwindled until they got to the point where there were no more of them left. They would have become extinct. You could think Neanderthals or a whole other species, or perhaps just a group of people who all had similar slight differences in their genetic makeup that made them less likely to survive and prosper. Either way, the environment they experienced at that time was not perfect for them and they fell by the wayside in the genetic race for survival.

However, as you and I are still around, along with billions of others just like us, the environment that our ancestors were exposed to was just right! It's like Goldilocks. Each time a slight variation in our genetic recipe book led to an advantage, there was a greater chance of our particular genome surviving long enough to reproduce. Each time a similar variation led to a disadvantage, there was more chance of that group of people becoming extinct.

Over many hundreds of thousands of years, this led to a gradual but constant improvement in our recipe book, such that we became the most dominant species on the planet and have since colonised virtually every corner of the world. That's how evolution works... a constant improvement to our genome shaped by the environment we find ourselves in over many thousands of years. Again, remember whenever you read "environment" in this book, think of everything your cells are exposed to, both internally and externally, physically, chemically and emotionally. Animals that have not been able to adapt to their environment, such as when there has been a sudden shift through rapid and extreme climate change, or the disappearance of a food type they rely on, will usually become extinct.

That's great news for you, however, as you've made it this far! You are the front runner; the leader in the genetic race to thrive. All those thousands of generations that went before you and that you are a direct descendant of, have left you with a near-perfect set of genes to thrive in good health, leading a long, happy, productive life. You got the golden ticket!

I love the pure, simplistic logic of it. Evolution. The elephant in the room here, though, is that why, if you have a perfect set of instructions, are you so likely, according to the statistics, to die from a chronic illness such as cancer, heart disease, diabetes, Alzheimer's and the like? How can all these so-called genetic illnesses be present if we've evolved to survive and thrive? Some people would have you believe it's because your genes have mutated and that you are flawed in some way. It's a faulty gene and there's nothing you can do about it, so why bother? It's just bad luck.

Well, the truth is your genes haven't changed for 40,000 years or so. Your genetic material is the same, give or take some slight variations, as the cavemen and women who lived in the wild tens of thousands of years ago. If you took a new-born baby from 40,000 years ago and transported him or her through time to today, that baby would grow up exactly the same as all the other babies who are born now. They'd be indistinguishable. Their genomes are the same.

So, if our genes are the same, something else must have changed. It's the environment we exist in. It's the chemicals we're exposed to, the foods we eat (or don't eat!) and the types of physical activity we engage in. It's the thoughts we have and the communities we live in.

There has been a fairly rapid change in the environment that modern humans have created for themselves over the past 10,000 years or so, and an incredible acceleration of those changes over the past 100 years. These changes have taken place at a faster rate than evolution can accommodate. There was no farming of crops or animals 10,000 years ago. All the foods that were eaten were gathered from the plants, trees and bushes that grew in the wild. We ate meat and fish but these lived in the wild, eating their own natural diet, and it was hard work to hunt them. We didn't eat grains such as wheat, rice and oats as, without machinery, they are hard to harvest and process to make them edible and it would have taken a lot of energy to do so. If we hunted an animal, we didn't tie it up and milk it. We killed it and ate the meat. If it happened to be nursing its young at the time, we may have drunk the contents of its udders whilst preparing the meat, but that would only have been an occasional food source rather than a constant supply. We needed to gather and hunt as many calories as possible with the quickest pay-off in terms of foods to eat just to survive, as living in the wild is tough.

Only once we began to get smarter about planting seeds to grow more food, and were able to domesticate animals to help with the labour-intensive nature of early farming, did the agricultural revolution begin. We still had the genes of our hunter-gatherer ancestors but had begun to quickly change the environment that we exposed them to in terms of the foods we ate and the kinds of activities we did. Still, all the foods were natural and it was very physical work to cultivate them. The huge advantage this brought those early farmers, though, was that their food supply became more plentiful and reliable. And once they'd created efficient ways of processing grains to make them edible, they were able to store foods for whenever they were needed. Grains, once milled and cooked, are an excellent source of energy and can be stored for a long time to be eaten when all the other crops have been used up. We've only been eating them for a relatively short period of time, though, from an evolutionary point of view, and since we have, our average height has fallen and a whole raft of new diseases has appeared.

Fast forward to the early 20th century. Prior to this, everything had been organic as no chemical pesticides or fertilisers existed. All foods were cooked from scratch as there were no ready meals or short cuts. No animals were intensively reared, living in confined spaces, overfed and given drugs to make them put on weight as fast as possible and, for the vast majority of us, daily life was still physically tough.

Now, the norm is to grow fruits and vegetables with chemical fertilisers and pesticides, and the majority of the animals we eat have led anything but a natural life. We drink huge quantities of sugary or artificially sweetened drinks, laced with weird chemical colours and flavours. Most of our foods come from brightly coloured packages produced in huge factories, where nutritional content is very low down the list of priorities because any corporation's job is actually to make money. They're not buying the best quality organic ingredients they can find and treating them with care to maximise the nutrients on your plate. Their main focus is producing a food product at as low a cost as they can that will stay edible in the warehouses and on supermarket shelves for as long as possible to maximise their profits.

Most of us are very sedentary, sitting for long periods of time in unnatural positions and rarely getting out of breath or expending energy to any great degree. Prolonged emotional stress, isolation and fear are commonplace, whether it be from the commute to work in the morning or office politics, the neighbour you don't get along with, or the constant bombardment in the media of death, destruction and scaremongering that we're exposed to.

You and all your family have the exact genes of a hunter-gatherer, perfectly adapted to the environment they were exposed to 10,000 years ago, but your current environment couldn't be more different. We are wild animals living in captivity, willingly isolated from the environment we are perfectly adapted to thrive in, but we are told that our illnesses are genetic. If you take any animal out of the wild and put it in a cage, forcing it to live in a way not congruent with the requirements of its genetic code, it will get ill. Many zoo animals develop illnesses that don't exist in their cousins left living a natural life in the wild, yet we still call them genetic conditions. What's changed? The environment! They'll be fed some similar foods to those in the wild (although they'll now have been grown using artificial fertilisers, processed and have added preservatives) but they won't have had to search and forage for them. Their climate will be different. They'll be told when to go to sleep, when to wake up and won't live in the same social groups. They won't have the freedom to roam, explore and build shelter. Is it any wonder we're so ill?

Shamefully, you and I are led to believe that the only option is to wait for illness and then get a lifetime of treatment to try to keep ourselves alive, all the while living in fear that we might succumb. We've heard that eating a healthy diet might help or that losing weight is a good idea; that lifestyle has a huge influence over our health. But does anyone actually believe the advice? I don't think they do. If they did and they took action, deaths from chronic illnesses would be falling, not rising as they are still doing. The rates of chronic lifestyle illnesses were very low three generations ago. They still existed but the numbers were tiny in comparison to today.

Some reports tell us we're living longer and that average life expectancy is rising. However, don't be fooled by this for two reasons. The first is that most people will spend the last ten years or so of their lives in a state of perpetual illness, surviving only because of the multiple medications they are prescribed. The second reason is that, as the term suggests, it's the "average" that is rising. The average is obviously calculated by adding together all the ages of the people at the time they died, and then dividing that number by the number of dead people. That number can be influenced by a wide range of factors, from infant mortality rates to protection against harsh weather conditions. It doesn't mean we're getting healthier as a society. And yes, perhaps we are living a little longer now, but if being around for longer and therefore having more of a chance of getting sick was the reason for the ever-increasing rates, why are younger and younger people developing and dying from these diseases? Tragically, children get cancer. Adult-onset diabetes had to be renamed Type 2 diabetes as younger and younger people were developing it.

Like me, you may remember news stories many years ago about the wildlife in our rivers and waterways dying out. Fish would either not be able to reproduce or would wash up on the banks, dead with weird tumours. The birds and other animals that ate those fish would also suffer illness and their numbers would begin to fall. At any point, did anyone claim that the fish were dying because of genetic illnesses? Did they attempt to decode their genome and point to a gene, calling it the "gill cancer" gene or "fin cancer" gene? And then did they raise millions of pounds to carry out research into drugs that could be given to the fish to treat their diseases? Of course not! That would have been ludicrous and laughable. So what caused all the wildlife to die if it wasn't genetic? It was the toxic pollution that was being allowed to be dumped into the river upstream. It was one aspect of the environment the fish were living in.

The animal species known as human is just the same, but we are told it's because of faulty genes or bad luck that we're ill. We cleaned up the rivers and the fish got better, so now it's time to improve *our* environment.

We still haven't truly made the connection between lifestyle and disease. It's become the new normal to develop cancer, diabetes and the like; everyone knows someone who is either currently fighting it or has died from it. Public opinion is that it's inevitable that something like that will get you and your best hope is to pray for early detection and a miracle cure. We all look sorrowfully at the victim and think, "Oh dear, well, what can you do? Thank goodness it's not me."

This used to be the way with lung cancer. For years the link between smoking and lung cancer was talked about but denied. Doctors used to promote cigarette smoking as a way to relax and be calm and smokers used to deny the link because they didn't want to stop their pleasurable habit. Only since the late 20th century has it been widely accepted that, if someone has lung cancer, they were probably exposed to cigarette smoke as either a smoker or a passive smoker for an extended period of time.

It's not so accepted for the other major killers, though. Type 2 diabetes is a failure of the body to produce enough insulin to transport sugar from the bloodstream for use in your muscles or to be stored as fat for later use. When you eat a meal, your digestive system breaks down the food into its constituent parts in a form that can be absorbed and used by the body. This will be to give you energy but also nutrients essential to health. One constituent part is sugar in various forms, which comes from the carbohydrates in your food. This is absorbed into the bloodstream but must be controlled within a strict band between a low and high level, as moving outside this band is very dangerous to you. In simple terms, if you eat a meal high in carbohydrates, your stomach will dump a lot of sugar into your blood. Your pancreas will then be signalled to produce insulin to cope with it. However, if you repeatedly eat high carbohydrate meals over a long period of time, it takes more and more insulin to deal with the same amount of sugar. You put on weight as the excess sugar is stored as body fat, very often around the midriff. You begin to develop what is termed "insulin resistance" as it's more and more difficult to "push" the sugar into your tissues, and it takes more and more insulin to do it. This will eventually lead to not enough insulin being able to be produced, dangerously high levels of blood sugar and a diagnosis of Type 2 diabetes.

Now, you may be aware that, in its early stages, the usual course of action is to follow a strict diet to lose weight, as for some reason the excess body fat is seen as a cause of the diabetes rather than a result of the prolonged, excessive sugar intake. So, you're given a diet sheet that features low-fat foods such as skimmed milk and fat-free dairy products, "healthy" whole grains such as brown rice and bread, and are told to avoid cakes and puddings etc. Well, the last one makes perfect sense as desserts are obviously high in table sugar, but to promote eating grains makes absolutely no sense at all. When your body digests grain-based foods such as pasta, rice and breads, they are all broken down in your stomach and the high carbohydrate constituent enters your bloodstream as sugar. Just what your body can't deal with in your diabetic state!

Similarly, when dairy products are consumed, your body is signalled to produce insulin (but the reason is not fully understood), which again puts your overworked pancreas under stress. The diet often leads to weight loss if it can be sustained, as it's not very pleasurable. However, the patient will always have Type 2 diabetes as they still can't produce the insulin required to properly cope with the sugars in their blood. They'll then likely be prescribed a drug called Metformin and become another lifelong customer of the pharmaceutical industry.

If the link between carbohydrate consumption and diabetes had been truly made and accepted by the public, the diet would be very different. But there will be more on this in a later chapter. To illustrate how little education the general public have on this particular illness, I was amazed to see a charity raffle prize in my local supermarket last Christmas. Tickets were being sold by a well-meaning member of staff to raise money for a diabetes charity – and what was the first prize? You guessed it, a hamper filled with cakes, Christmas pudding, chocolates and sweets! And if you still can't see the irony, imagine a similar raffle in aid of a lung cancer charity with a first prize of 100 cigarettes! No one would possibly consider that to be acceptable but cakes and sweets in aid of diabetes were fine. After all, it's just a bit of cake, isn't it? Go on, it's Christmas!

While it's true that not every single person who smokes develops lung cancer and not everyone who eats excessive sugars will become diabetic, the odds of doing so are greatly shifted by living the necessary lifestyle. Bad habits by me could lead to a particular chronic illness but the same bad habits by you may not. You could get a whole different illness. It's the slight genetic differences between you and me that will result in the particular disease. And what's the common factor here? It's not the genes. They don't cause the illness. It's the bad choices and bad habits; it's the things that are missing from your life that your body requires for health; it's the constant barrage of toxic things that you put into your body that it has to deal with and remove. It's your lifestyle and the subsequent environment that this creates for you.

It's true that some genes have been labelled as the breast cancer gene and the like, and that these can be inherited from your parents, but that doesn't mean you'll get the disease. Roughly two thirds of the women who carry breast cancer genes never develop breast cancer, so we shouldn't be tricked into calling it a genetic condition. The genes were passed to them by their parents but they didn't get the disease. They didn't create the environment that encourages a tumour to grow in their breast tissue.

However, what is also passed down through families are habits and choices; you'll likely eat and live in similar ways to your parents and if these habits created the environment needed for chronic illness in them, then the odds are that's what will happen for you. I may have the hangover gene but if I don't do the things that cause a hangover, namely drink excess alcohol, I won't get a hangover!

There is another option: prevention. Prevention means never putting your body into a situation for a prolonged period of time that it can't deal with. It means making sensible, logical choices, based on sound, reasoned arguments. Your body is a perfectly built ecosystem, constantly trying to move you towards a state of health in order for you to thrive and pass on your genes to the next generation. It isn't flawed and it doesn't just randomly go wrong. Failures only occur through frequent or repeated differences between what it needs and what you provide it with. Stop thinking of illness as a need for a drug or magical herb and start acknowledging that it appears because you've either not given your body what it needs for health, or you've given it too much crap to deal with for too long! Headaches are not caused by a paracetamol deficiency and diabetes is not a lack of Metformin in your system.

I'm not saying that we all need to go back to living in the wild and forgo all our modern comforts. We just need to consciously think about the choices we make in daily life. Is what I am about to do compatible with how my ancestors lived? Are my genes expecting this or will it be unknown to them? Is this going to move me closer to health or closer to sickness? You don't have to become a caveman but there are loads of logical and easy things you can do to improve your chances of a productive life of good health, and reduce the chances of spending the last few years of your shortened life in fear and ill health.

The main focus of the following chapters is on what is required for maximum prevention, from a logical and NATURAL perspective:

N - Nutrition
A - Alignment and Posture
T - Thoughts
U - Unsafe Toxins
R - Rest
A - Activity
L - Love and Connection

All these elements form the environment that every cell of your body experiences on a minute-by-minute basis. Whenever I talk about environment in this book, it is this that I'm referring to. Everything you do can either be classed as something that moves you closer to, or further away from, a healthy environment. Do you choose to eat a piece of fruit as a snack or a chocolate bar? The fruit is filled with vitamins and minerals and, hopefully, no pesticides. The chocolate bar is mainly sugar in various forms with virtually no nutritional value, and possibly contains many things that don't occur in nature. Choosing the chocolate not only gives your body crap to deal with but also deprives it of the nutrients that would have been in the fruit.

Do you take the stairs or the escalator? Taking the stairs will obviously involve a little exercise. It will require your legs to lift your body weight several times, stretching your hips in the process and strengthening your thighs; it will elevate your heart rate; it will improve your insulin response by burning the carbohydrate stored in your muscles to help regulate your blood sugar. Taking the escalator will do nothing but deprive you of the positive impact of the stairs.

Every one of your 75 trillion cells is influenced in some way by all seven of the aforementioned areas, either positively or negatively, and the choices you make are completely up to you. Unless you've made great choices in all these areas, at the same time, repeatedly over a reasonable period, you haven't yet felt what it is to be truly healthy. Remember, health is not just the absence of symptoms or a disease. True health is every one of the cells in your personal ecosystem functioning as it should, at the same time.

CHAPTER 2

Nutrition

THE NATURAL DIET FOR THE HUMAN ANIMAL

The foods you've been told to eat over many years have probably changed, with official guidelines and government recommendations gradually moving. The media can often over-sensationalise or misreport the findings of the latest nutritional study or research in order to create bold headlines and sell more papers, and this can influence your food choices. It's become very confusing knowing what's good and what isn't anymore under the barrage of contradictory information. The main driver behind the bulk of these conflicting bits of advice is often the desire for a company or industry sector to sell more of their products, as they're in the business of making money first and foremost, not healthier people. Remember that throughout reading this chapter; the packaging on foods, including the words used, colours chosen and ingredients emphasised, have all been selected by panels of highly paid and intelligent people, whose sole purpose is to get you to buy more of their stuff. That might seem obvious and completely innocent but repeatedly reading "low fat" or "no cholesterol" on the front of food packets, for instance, reinforces this message until it seems that it must be right because you see it everywhere.

From a logical point of view, there must be a natural diet for humans. We are just another animal species with specific requirements in terms of nutrition, along with every other animal that we share this planet with. What I need to eat for optimum health is going to be the same as you need. It's going to be the same as your great-great-great-great-grandparents needed for health and every one of the generations in your family tree for the past 40,000 years. You might disagree with this statement because of your current life experiences or on religious grounds but I urge you to read on.

Picture a game reserve in Africa. There are thousands of animals living in the wild and hundreds of different species. They're roaming around, searching for food and eating it. Do the wardens need to round up every giraffe, take blood samples and then carry out some genetic tests to determine what the correct diet for each individual giraffe is? Do they then prevent some giraffes from eating certain foods, or supplement their diet with something that none of the others eat depending on the results of their tests? Or do they just know what giraffes eat and that each one has the same requirements? The same goes for all other animals; there is a natural diet for them that is the same for all members of that species. It's what their genes have evolved to require and expect.

We are just another one of those animal species. To understand what our natural diet is, many people far smarter than I am have studied the fossil remains of our ancestors and written hundreds of scientific papers about it. They've also discovered and studied tribes of humans who still live in the wild in very remote places untouched by modern civilisation, free from all the illnesses that are commonplace in our societies.

Our foods are arguably the most important area of health, potentially having the most impact on our risk factors for chronic illness. Foods provide the source of fuel to keep your brain alive and your heart beating, but are also the only way to take in the building blocks to heal, grow and repair the body. We seem to concentrate more on the fuel aspect of foods in terms of calories but neglect the nutritional aspects. Calories are always listed first on the label and they are used to compare one food against another to rate its worth. The TV and other media often talk about low-calorie foods as if they're a great idea and what you should be choosing first. But, if you were living in the wild where foods were often scarce, it would make much more sense to search for and value high-calorie foods; foods that provide the best return in terms of energy compared to the effort it took to collect them. If you were out walking for miles and miles, climbing trees all day or chasing down an animal for meat, and all you found were a few bunches of celery and a very lean animal, whose skin you removed along with all the fat, you wouldn't necessarily survive for very long. You'd constantly be using more energy from your reserves than you were putting back in.

I think it much more likely that energy-dense foods were prized whenever they were available; that the fattier parts of an animal were the best as they provided the maximum energy return. That's not to say that our ancestors ate a very fatty diet. The animals they hunted for food would all have lived in the wild, obviously eating their own natural diet. As such, they would have been much more lean than the farmed animals we mainly eat today: the farmed animals that are purposely fed a diet designed to make them put on as much muscle and fat as possible and get them to a weight "ready for market" to maximise the farmer's profits.

However, this wouldn't have been the case if you happened to be an Eskimo, Inuit or belonged to some other indigenous population near the arctic. Their main food source for a large part of each year is whale meat and blubber, a food source very high in saturated fat with an equally high energy density. Based on one of the myths that have been drummed into us for so long, that saturated fat and cholesterol are bad for us, you would expect these people to be unhealthy, overweight and dying of heart disease. Not at all. These chronic illnesses are unheard of among these populations and they live very long, productive lives. Until, that is, they move to live in the modern, western, "civilised" world! They then start eating our diet of processed and unnatural foods and, hey presto, they begin to develop the diseases that kill us too: namely cancer, heart disease, diabetes, Alzheimer's etc.

But, wait a minute. We're told that it's the high cholesterol and saturated fat that are bad for us. Yet they just can't be! Time after time, study after study shows that there is no causal link between eating a diet high in saturated animal fats and the risk of heart disease, and that even the exact opposite is true: those who eat the highest amounts of saturated fats tend to have lower rates of heart disease.

The cholesterol myth first appeared in the late 1950s. I believe it has been responsible for a huge amount of unnecessary illness and suffering ever since, but has made a lot of people billions of pounds in profits. A researcher called Ancel Keys came up with a hypothesis linking the consumption of saturated fats and cholesterol with the rate of heart disease. It seemed to be logical at the time. Those with heart disease were found to have deposits of a fatty, cholesterol-containing plaque building up in their arteries, which gradually caused their blood pressure to rise and the flow of blood through their heart to fall, eventually starving the heart muscle of sufficient oxygen and causing a heart attack. So, it would seem logical to assume that if you were to eat a lot of cholesterol, it could be this that was clogging your arteries.

Keys needed to try to prove his hypothesis, so he carried out a study comparing the amount of cholesterol in the diets of inhabitants of several countries and the likelihood of heart disease in the same people. He found a correlation between a number of these countries, including the UK, Australia, Canada and the USA. It seemed that the countries whose inhabitants ate the most cholesterol-containing foods also had the most heart disease and this is what he published in his research. However, what didn't get mentioned in the media, and has only recently started to be talked about, is that he ignored several countries that he studied where the exact opposite was true, because they didn't suit his theory. Countries such as Norway and Holland had high saturated fat consumption but low rates of heart disease. There were also countries, like Chile, that had low cholesterol consumption but still had high heart disease! If Keys's theory was to be believed, these countries were a problem. So he discounted them, ignored them and published his research without including them! And the myth began.

Keys's edited findings were widely reported in the media and gained acceptance because the people who developed heart disease were often overweight or obese. They had high body fat and eating fat makes you fat, doesn't it? Therefore, it must be true that eating cholesterol-containing saturated fats leads to being fat and then to heart disease.

Thankfully, there is now a vast quantity of good science that disproves this. Unfortunately, however, because the cholesterol myth has been around for so long, it's still widely considered to be true and forms part of official government guidelines on a healthy diet. From a logical point of view, it makes absolutely no sense that a food highly prized by thousands of generations of our ancestors, that they ate whenever it was available and evolved to thrive on, would actually be the cause of an illness. If that had been true, those who ate most of it would have likely died earlier and become extinct, leaving behind the people who didn't eat it to grow and thrive. Their genome would have been selected through the evolutionary process to prosper. But that didn't happen.

The saturated fat myth has gained great acceptance through multiple means and our governments, healthcare providers and food industries are all to blame. It's very lazy "science" to say that eating fat makes you fat and fat people tend to be sicker, so eating low fat must be healthier. This is what comes from the government and is then promulgated by the medical professions. As much as you would like to think that your GP is highly educated and an expert in nutrition, in general, GPs really aren't. They have very little education in this area whilst studying medicine, the clue there being that they are studying *medicine*, not *health*. The two things are very different. If you're lucky, he or she might have been interested enough to keep abreast of the research as it appeared and remained open minded to any ideas that bucked the accepted knowledge.

But your GP is incredibly busy and has to be focused on the symptoms you present with, in the few minutes allocated to each appointment. The main tools they have in their box are a drug or a surgical procedure cleverly designed to alleviate the symptoms you're complaining of. So that's what they provide you with. Coaching someone towards better lifestyle choices is difficult and time-consuming, and all too often the patient doesn't want to hear that anyway. They want a quick fix. "Give me a pill to make it go away." Is it any wonder your GP doesn't keep up to date with nutritional information, yet doctors are held up on a pedestal as the fountains of all health knowledge? If your GP said it, it must be true. They have what is termed "cultural authority", whereby whatever they say is usually accepted by whoever hears it and no one can sway their belief in it. If your GP disseminates incorrect government guidelines to you because that's all they've got time to do, it then becomes true in your eyes.

To further reinforce this new truth, food manufacturers think, "We can make some money here." So, they begin producing a vast array of products to sit on the supermarket shelves, in perfectly designed packaging, with the same words on that you heard from your GP: "Low cholesterol", "Low saturated fat" or just "diet". These must be healthy choices because my GP said so. The adverts are all over the

TV and other media too, constantly reinforcing the same message, so surely it's true? You rarely see the words "saturated fats" without the words "artery-clogging" before them and the myth becomes more and more ingrained. The population is getting fatter so we're told that we should eat less fat. The cholesterol myth is widely believed and fat contains cholesterol – so it must be good advice to avoid fat.

Unfortunately, however, there are other ways to become fat. Eating grains, for instance, such as wheat in its many forms, will make you fat. In fact, anything that elevates your blood sugar excessively will encourage your body to quickly remove the sugar and convert it to fat for future use, unless you happen to be running a marathon at the time! When the farmer wants to fatten up his cows, encouraging them to put on weight and grow quickly so they're ready for market, what does he feed them? He feeds them grains! Grains are not the natural diet for cows, or sheep or pigs for that matter, and eating them makes them ill and fat relatively quickly. They cause them gastrointestinal distress and the animals produce large quantities of methane. If eating fat was the quickest way for them to put on weight, that's what farmers would feed them, but it isn't. Grain-fed cattle (meaning cows on a high carbohydrate diet) often have high levels of intramuscular fat, and this is prized by chefs and butchers, who call it "marbling". The fat within the muscle gives the meat additional flavour and can help keep it moist during cooking but it's not an indication of a healthy animal. Guess what? Grain-fed humans also have higher levels of intramuscular fat! So instead of having strong, powerful muscles to move you around, you have a mixture of muscle and fat, which is weaker.

Cholesterol is an extremely important substance in your body and whatever level it is at right now, it's the appropriate level for you and your current environment. It's vital to healing and repair. So, if you find yourself being chased by a tiger through the jungle, which I would imagine is quite stressful, your blood pressure will rise to carry enough oxygenated blood around your body, and your cholesterol levels will naturally increase as your body gets ready in case there is a need to heal a wound. Fortunately, this doesn't mean that you need to have eaten enough eggs at the right time, just before the tiger comes to get you, as your body creates its own cholesterol. The cholesterol in the foods you eat has very little to do with the levels measured in your blood. Your body is regulating the amount all the time so that it's appropriate for your current environment.

The problem here is that we can often find ourselves in a state of long-term stress for a variety of reasons, whether emotional or physical, but your body doesn't really see a difference. All it knows is that your current situation is a stressful one, potentially leading to harm, and so the necessary ingredients for healing and repair could be important very soon. It therefore raises your blood pressure and manufactures more cholesterol in readiness.

However, because we've made a terrible mistake and assumed that high cholesterol in your blood is what leads to the cholesterol deposits in your arteries, the medical answer to this is to give you drugs to artificially lower your measured cholesterol levels. Statins are the single most over-prescribed drug on the market and an enormous money-maker for the pharmaceutical industry. Your doctor checks your cholesterol level and determines it is "too high", so prescribes a statin. The statin artificially forces the level in your blood lower but your body knows where the level should be based on your current environment, stress and anxiety levels. So, your body tries to raise the cholesterol in your blood to bring it back to where it should be.

You go back to the GP a few weeks later to be checked. They measure the levels and, finding them to still be "too high", they increase the dose of your statins until eventually your body can't compensate anymore and the levels settle at a level that your GP decides is "healthy"! No one has checked your lifestyle or emotional state. No one has enquired about the tigers that are currently chasing you and how they could be removed. Your lifestyle stays the same and, inevitably, you still die of heart disease at about the same age as you would have done but now you have low cholesterol.

The studies don't lie. There is so little evidence to back up this statin myth that it's a travesty that they're still being prescribed in such huge quantities. Of course, if you challenge your GP about this, they'll probably say that statins are safe and save lives and you'll probably assume they're right as they have the "cultural authority". They'll tell you that the research they've seen backs it up, but I'll bet that research was conducted by the drug company that's manufacturing the statins in the first place and making an enormous amount of money from them. And the studies from the drug companies will state something like: the patients had high cholesterol. We gave them this statin and then they had lower cholesterol. Therefore, their risk profile for heart disease has lowered. Fortunately, only a few people died as a result of the side effects of the statins, or of the other drugs they had to take to deal with the side effects of the statins, so we'll still claim a success!

The problem is, the patient's lifestyle probably remains the same, so they'll still die of a heart attack but with a nice low cholesterol number in their medical records. It's not the high cholesterol that killed them but the lifestyle choices they made that led to their body raising their cholesterol levels. You can't blame the cholesterol.

Now, I'm not trying to say that you can eat as much fat as you want and there will be no adverse consequences, such as weight gain, as that would be silly, and fats that don't occur in nature should be avoided at all costs. Unnatural fats, such as vegetable oils, became prevalent as a result of the cholesterol myth and the fear of saturated fats, but they are undoubtedly an unhealthy fat. They're usually chemically extracted and very high in omega 6 fatty acids which, when ingested to excess, will cause inflammation throughout your body. But we've been told they don't contain "artery-clogging saturated fats" so we've all believed they must be healthy. They're usually used for frying but become even more hazardous when heated to high temperatures as toxic compounds are created. In fact, all fats are damaged with high heat but, ironically (and probably logically), the ones that are least affected are saturated fats such as butter, lard and coconut oil.

Taking in an excess of calories in any form will eventually lead to weight gain, but avoiding eating fat and focusing on grain-based carbohydrates will definitely trigger your body to store the excess energy as body fat.

However, grains are not just a source of carbohydrate-based energy. They also contain things called lectins that have been shown to disrupt proper digestion in your gut and stop you from absorbing nutrients from the other foods you've eaten. Grains are effectively the seeds from different varieties of grass plants. In nature, for them to become widespread and cultivate other areas of ground, they have evolved a clever means of being distributed by other animals. When an animal eats the grass plant, including the seeds, the stalk is digested in the stomach but the seeds pass through the digestive system and are then deposited, along with the animal's poop, somewhere else, ready to grow into a new plant.

The reason the seeds are not digested and remain intact is the protection given by the lectins. This ability to disrupt digestion is what causes us the problems, as we've not evolved to handle seeds in the same way as other animals. For us to utilise grains as an energy source, they must be processed before consumption, meaning they must be dried, separated from the plant, milled into flour, turned into a dough and then cooked before eating. It's relatively easy for this to happen now because of industrial machinery, but imagine if you were doing it manually. If you had to hunt and gather all your foods to ensure survival, would you spend a long time manually picking the seeds from stalks of grass until you'd collected enough, then drying them for a while? To make them edible, you'd then have to pound them or grind them by hand to turn them into flour, which is very labour-intensive work, mix them with water and cook them. At that point, you'd get your energy source from the bread you'd made. Meanwhile, your neighbour has been out, has trapped or hunted an animal, picked a few fruits from the trees or dug up some roots, and has a meal ready much more quickly, having used less energy in the process. They also have a greater chance of survival as a result.

Again, I'm not saying that our relatively modern, hunter-gatherer ancestors never ate grains, as there is evidence that this started about 10,000 years ago. And a big advantage of grains as a food source is they are fairly easy to store for later use if you were to find yourself unable to hunt or locate your usual food sources, for instance in a harsh winter. But your genes were not shaped by relying on grain-based foods for the majority of the time.

Perhaps you think you don't eat a lot of grains but look around you at the supermarket checkout the next time you're there. Breads, pastries, pasta, rice and cereals are all grains and form the bulk of most people's weekly shop and hence their calorie intake. Not to mention a huge array of other foods in brightly coloured packaging, with numerous grain-based ingredients; just check the list of ingredients on the side. So not only do you create your meals around grain-based foods, causing yourself digestive problems, high blood sugar and encouraging fat storage, but you also then starve your body of the nutrients it actually needs from the vegetables and plant-based foods you're not eating because the grains have replaced them! It's a double whammy of devastation.

The disruption to digestion is not the only negative effect of grain consumption, though. Prolonged consumption leads to damage of the stomach and intestinal wall that comes in various forms. If you're lucky, you "only" develop leaky gut, whereby the holes in the lining of your digestive tract that allow properly digested nutrients to be absorbed into the blood stream become too big. This allows substances to get through into your bloodstream that wreak havoc with many of the systems in your body. Hormonal changes can occur and widespread low-level inflammation throughout your body, leading to arthritic changes in your joints and subsequent joint pain, allergies and a variety of other problems. If you're unlucky, you'll develop full-blown Crohn's disease or ulcerative colitis, leading to permanent damage to the villi that form the lining of the gut wall, terrible stomach cramps and near permanent intestinal gas and diarrhoea. Not at all pleasant.

If our particular species of human animal had been eating grains for hundreds of thousands of years and had hardly touched meat, vegetables or fruit, our genome would now be very different to what it is. We'd have evolved into a different species and eating bread, pasta and rice would be all we would need to do for health, as these would have been the foods that had shaped our DNA. We'd be able to properly digest and utilise the nutrients in the grains to nourish our bodies, and the lectins wouldn't affect our digestion. There would be no need for meat, fish, plants and fruits and eating these in abundance would make us very ill. Can you imagine feeding a zebra meat and fruit, for example? Or how about a lion living on vegetables? Would they become healthier or sicker? Would they even eat the foods at all and, if not, starve to death? Their genes have been shaped by the diets that are right for them, just as ours have.

A pivotal moment for me personally with regard to grain consumption occurred in my mid-thirties. Since the age of around 12, I'd had terrible hay fever (an allergy to various tree and grass pollens) for the bulk of the summer months and nothing seemed to help. Each summer I'd take the next anti-histamine that had been developed in the hope that I'd get some relief from my constantly running nose, itchy eyes and sore ear canals. I permanently carried around a damp handkerchief, using two or three every day, and sneezed violently all the time. The treatments available didn't really help much, occasionally giving a little temporary relief, and I suffered the usual side effects of tiredness and lethargy. Even in the months outside my hay fever season, I'd occasionally get a seemingly random bad day that would come out of the blue and leave me fed up, shaking and exhausted.

This carried on every year until, at about 35, I began to be exposed to the health experts who have shaped the past ten years of my life. Whilst attending the seminars of Dr James Chestnut, I learned about the negative impact of a diet based on grains, so my wife and I decided it would be a good idea to experiment and cut them out of our diet. This wasn't done with the intention of treating my hay fever or any other condition, as I hadn't even made that connection. Besides, it was autumn when we started so I had no symptoms.

Time went by and we found it relatively easy to eat in this way. Then the summer months arrived. I knew that my hay fever season was approaching as it had caused me misery for over 20 years at that point - but the symptoms never appeared. I kept waiting to wake up with the tell-tale tickle in the back of my throat and nose but I went through the whole summer with nothing at all. It wasn't that it had got less frequent or the symptoms had reduced; after 23 years of having it for the same three months in midsummer, it just never arrived.

I wondered if it could be related to my dietary changes, so I spoke to an ENT specialist whose care I'd been under previously. He confirmed to me that it was probably because of the pro-inflammatory nature of grains. I was still allergic to the pollen, he surmised, but without the elevated background inflammation caused by the grains, my allergy wasn't enough to tip the scales into noticeable symptoms. Whatever the reason, I didn't care. It had been the first summer I remembered without people asking me if I had a cold, without a damp hanky in my pocket and without feeling exhausted at the end of every day.

Our eating habits stayed the same for a few years until, one year, old habits began to creep back in and wheat-based bread and pastry became an occasional and then a regular treat. Summer came around and I had my hay fever symptoms again, so I got back to avoiding the grains and the symptoms disappeared. I have no idea if the explanation I've pieced together to describe the connection is accurate but, to be honest, it doesn't matter. I just know that if I avoid grains, and it seems to be predominantly wheat, I don't get hayfever.

What this made me think was, if my allergy symptoms are a visible sign of the problems caused by eating wheat, what other internal, unseen things are slowly happening as a result of chronic inflammation? What are the effects on other people who don't have obviously visible symptoms? I could easily write an entire chapter on this topic but instead, I would highly recommend you read two further books on the subject, *Wheat Belly* by cardiologist Dr William Davis (Harper Thorsons, 2015) and *Grain Brain* by neurologist Dr David Perlmutter (Yellow Kite, 2014).

The foods that your ancestors ate were naturally occurring, alive and needed very little, if any, processing to make them edible. They were covered in natural bacteria, enzymes and yeasts that all helped to digest them in your stomach and make the nutrients available for use by your body. They weren't dead, sterile products that had been heavily processed in a factory and filled with preservatives and additives to improve their shelf life. They were whole foods; not extracts of foods or foods with a particular demonised ingredient removed (such as fat) but then replaced with another weird-sounding array of ingredients that are hard to pronounce and intended to make them palatable. Roughly half the cells that make up you live in your gut and are not at all human. They are bacteria that you can't possibly function without and that allow you to digest and extract a wide variety of nutrients and then synthesize others that you need for health. Eating a diet of dead, processed, sterile foods can't possibly result in health as you need to feed and replenish these beneficial bacteria to enable them to carry on doing the vital work they do for you.

The community of bacteria in your gut is termed your "microbiome" and you must take great care of it if you are to enjoy good health. There are numerous sources of beneficial bacteria to help replenish it, such as fermented foods like sauerkraut and kimchi, or just a good quality probiotic supplement. You must also give these bacteria the foods they need for survival in the form of prebiotics, such as the fibre in plants and vegetables.

When babies are still in their mothers' wombs, they are completely sterile. There are no bacteria around them or inside them at all. When they are born through a normal vaginal-birth process, their skin and mouths become alive with the bacteria contained within their mothers' birth canals. It's the most important meal they ever get as it begins to colonise their gut with the necessary bacteria to properly digest milk and feed their immune system. To illustrate the importance of this first meal, numerous studies have shown that vaginal-birth children have a much better health status than children born by caesarean section at various age milestones through their formative years, with less likelihood of developing illnesses such as asthma, allergies and Type 1 diabetes.

When in conversation with people and the subject of diet comes up, I explain that I eat virtually no wheat, rice, pasta and bread, not to mention very little dairy, such as milk, cream, butter or cheese. I am always asked the same question: "Well, what do you eat?" To them, it sounds as though there's nothing left, as these foods form the bulk of most westerners' diets.

So what do I eat? Naturally reared animals, eggs, wild fish, plants and roots that grow in the ground and fruits and nuts that grow on trees. Foods that require minimal processing, if any, to make them edible, can be eaten raw or just need gentle cooking. It's very simple! These are the foods that your ancestors ate in abundance and that have shaped your genes. They are the foods that your body is constantly crying out for to heal, grow and repair. Initially, it can sound limiting but it really isn't. It's a huge array of foods that can be used to create an enormous selection of meals. Admittedly, if you generally buy pre-packaged foods, it can take a little time to get used to and you're going to have to actually cook from scratch, but the benefits are enormous. Your meals won't be bland because you'll use herbs and spices to flavour them, which not only add interest but also deliver further nutritional benefits. You'll know exactly what you're putting into your body and none of it will sound as if it's from a chemical laboratory.

I tend to buy my meat from the farmers' market and freeze it. I love being able to ask the person who's serving me about how the animals are reared, what they are fed and if they have any drugs routinely administered. (Try doing that in a supermarket!) The proprietors are usually more than happy to discuss it with you (as long as there isn't a queue building as a result!), as you'll find they have a genuine passion for what they do and it matters to them. That's why they've decided to take this route to get their products to the consumer.

I try to avoid buying farmed fish and only choose wild, sustainably caught seafood. Farmed fish are kept in extremely unnatural conditions, often swimming around in a concentration of their own waste and fed an unnatural diet. They're not able to lead a natural life so are effectively ill and stressed, leading to you eating a sick animal.

I try to buy organic fruits and vegetables whenever they're available, because this means they've been grown naturally without the addition of artificial fertilisers and pesticides. Otherwise the residues of these chemicals are then contained within your food and your body has to deal with them. I know there have been a lot of arguments for and against organic foods in the media, and a while back I remember reading that it had been proved there were no more nutrients in one compared to the other. The naysayers then all claimed this was proof that organic was a waste of time and money. However, for me, it has never been about the relative nutrient density, but more about toxin avoidance. I think one problem is that organic and non-organic look the same on the shelves, although non-organic fruits and vegetables can often look bigger as they've been artificially enhanced by the chemicals used during production.

But consider this little thought experiment: you've been growing some carrots in your garden for many months, entirely organically. You know that the soil was in great condition beforehand and has never seen any pesticides, weedkillers or petrochemical-based fertilisers. You've tended your plot every day and seen your seeds grow into beautiful vegetables. The time comes when you're going to harvest some and cook them to feed yourself and your children. You pull them up, clean off the soil and cook them in whatever way you've chosen. They're on the plates but, just before you serve them, someone comes along and, onto one plate, they sprinkle a tiny amount of pesticide and a similar tiny amount of artificial fertiliser. "It's OK," they say. "The amounts are within safe levels, similar to the residues left in conventionally grown carrots." Would you still want to eat the one with the residues? Would you pass the plate to your child for them to eat? Probably not, because now your perception has changed. It's no longer just a carrot from the bag you bought at the supermarket. It's a carrot with poisons added, just the same as the conventional one on the shelves, but the difference is you *saw* the chemicals being added.

Soils that are constantly fertilised with chemical fertilisers and sprayed with weedkillers and pesticides don't grow healthy crops. The soil becomes depleted of real nutrients, which leads to the fruit and vegetables being laced with toxic substances that your body has to deal with. The crops look the same as organically grown, and nutritionally they have similar levels of vitamins and minerals, but they also come packaged with a toxic burden that your body has to process. Over time, certain elements of these toxic substances bio-accumulate in your body and can lead to all kinds of unpleasant illnesses. We're told that the amounts present are "within safe levels" but how is that even determined? No one has done any lifelong trials comparing people who eat only conventionally grown crops with those who only ever eat organic. The so-called safe levels are inferred and calculated by the very people who manufacture the chemicals, and are based on relatively short-term exposure. They're also taken in isolation, assuming that no other toxic loads are present in your body at the same time from other sources.

I'm fortunate to live on the edge of a small village, very close to open countryside. There is a farm track at the end of my road that leads down to the river. It's a great place to walk or run. However, a couple of times I've managed to time my run with when the farmer is out spraying his crops and the wind has carried the spray across to me. On one occasion, I hadn't realised he was spraying until I became aware of a very strong smell, almost oily in nature. I looked across and, in the distance, I could see the tractor with its wide spray bars on and a cloud of mist following it behind. It began to make me cough and choke and my chest became suddenly tight and wheezy. I had to stop running and I noticed two dog walkers coming towards me, both having pulled the necks of their jumpers up over their noses and mouths to breathe through. I had to do the same and I turned back to get home as quickly as possible.

It was quite a shocking experience and I realised I'd probably be eating those crops laced with the strong-smelling chemical in the near future. Now, it might seem a little sensationalist to reference that experience with ingesting the same chemicals in the foods, but it's just accepted that you will take them in. After only eating them a few times, the residues are detectable in your urine and the tissues of your body. They're definitely in there and are virtually unavoidable in our western civilisation. The only thing you can do is to make conscious decisions to be aware of them and limit your exposure.

You should try to aim for as much free-range, naturally reared and naturally grown food as possible. Eating the foods that are in season at that time is also a good idea. It's no coincidence that higher carbohydrate (and therefore high sugar) foods encourage us to put on weight. Naturally occurring high sugar foods, such as fruits and starchy roots, generally appear in the autumn. In the past, eating an abundance of these would trigger the storage of this extra sugar as fat just before winter came, which would give you some energy reserves to call upon during those leaner times when food became scarce. It also explains to me why there is a health benefit to fasting for short periods of time, as it's natural for us. If your ancestors hadn't had this inbuilt ability, and eating high carbohydrate foods had led to them losing weight in autumn, they'd have lost a distinct advantage to their neighbours who were able to get through the winter using their stored fat. They would have had a lower chance of survival and could possibly have died out. It's evolution again!

Animals kept in unnatural conditions and fed an unnatural diet are not healthy. If you could see the different life being led by a naturally reared animal when compared to an intensively reared one, and could compare their relative health statuses, you would view the meat differently, just as in the carrot example. Unfortunately, all we tend to see is meat on the supermarket shelves and it all looks the same regardless of the animal's health status at the time it was slaughtered. However, the nutritional profile is very different. I'm sure you're aware of the health benefits of eating oily fish because of the omega 3 fats it contains. Well, did you know that properly reared meat from cows that eat their natural diet of grasses contains a high level of omega 3 oil too? Logically, there would have to have been other sources of it throughout evolution, as not all humans would have lived close to waterways containing oily fish.

Omega 3 fats are termed "essential fatty acids" as they can't be synthesised in the body but are needed for health, and the only way we can obtain them is through our diet. So, for humans who didn't live close to a supply of oily fish, the wild animals they hunted provided the source they needed. However, if you feed cattle on a diet of mainly grains, or even just feed them grains for the last few weeks of life to fatten them up for market, their flesh becomes depleted of omega 3 fats and, instead, rich in omega 6 fats that come from the grains they ate. Omega 6 fats in excess cause inflammation, not only in the cow but also in you once you eat the meat. It's another double whammy whereby you don't get sufficient omega 3s but instead become overloaded with omega 6s.

I think of foods as having three main functions. First, they are a source of energy and we measure that in calories. Low-energy foods wouldn't have been prized by your ancestors as much as high-energy ones. Energy is the immediate function of food to beat your heart, fuel your brain and keep you moving. For a large part of our existence on the planet, we've eaten our foods raw as they were picked from the trees or dug from the ground. This also includes meat which, if fresh, can be eaten raw. However, at some point in the very distant past, your ancestors discovered that heating the foods could make them easier to chew and digest, and taste better.

Simple cooking practices emerged that began to accelerate our evolution as they enabled us to obtain more calories in a shorter amount of time. Rather than chewing through tough, fibrous roots for hours and dealing with sinewy raw meats, which then took a lot more energy to digest through a much longer digestive tract, we could spend less time obtaining our energy because of the changes in the foods that cooking brings.

That leads on to the second function of food, which is to provide the nutrients needed to heal, grow and repair. All the millions of functions your body is constantly carrying out for you rely on having the necessary vitamins, minerals, fats and protein available whenever needed. If you're eating foods that are nutritionally poor, your body will potentially be starved of these nutrients and unable to function at its best. Injuries won't heal quickly or properly, hormones won't be manufactured in sufficient amounts and you'll live a poorer, worse life as a result.

The third function is to bring pleasure and satisfaction. This is often discounted or ignored in the nutritional textbooks but it is essential to the survival of any species. If animals didn't enjoy eating the diet that's right for them and instead, from birth, craved foods that were toxic, how could that species ever hope to survive and prosper?

It seems that, as a society, we believe that all healthy foods taste awful and it's miserable to eat well. Perhaps you've thought the same things yourself. There are two main issues at play here. The first is that a lot of the foods you've been led to believe are healthy, really aren't. And yes, they do taste unpleasant. Low-fat versions of foods never taste as good as their unprocessed, full-fat versions, anything with artificial sweeteners in is revolting to my taste buds and all breakfast cereals, unless covered in sugar, honey or chocolate (which they often already are), are truly like eating shredded cardboard!

The second thing at play is that, over the years, you've likely eaten food products that have been heavily processed and had lots of extra sugar or salt added, or the texture changed to make it unlike anything in nature but easier to eat. So you've forgotten how real food should taste. It takes a little time, but once you find out what healthy foods actually are and incorporate them into your diet, your cravings will change. The urge to eat a whole bar of chocolate will possibly never fully go away, but it becomes a much quieter voice in your head. Once you begin to picture these foods for what they really are, which is toxic, dead, highly processed, unnatural poisons, depleted of anything your body needs and full of things it has to deal with, you start to see them in a different light. You begin to crave real, whole foods and get pleasure from eating them.

A common complaint from parents is that they can't get their young child to eat vegetables, for instance, but the baby was born pre-programmed to want them. It has to have been! How many tiger cubs would survive if they were born not liking the taste of meat, or monkeys that didn't like fruit? What your child didn't have built in was a requirement for baby rice or other cooked cereal products that had to be flavoured or sweetened to make them palatable. Generally, what actually happens is we train our children to like foods other than those genetically required for health, until it gets to a point where they've lost the in-built craving for the right things. You'll also often find that the parents of the children who won't eat fruit and vegetables don't eat fruit and vegetables themselves, and instead have fed their children things like chips, crisps and sweets. Is it any wonder they won't now switch!

Depending on your current diet, making changes can be stressful to the point where you might be thinking you can't do it. Having someone tell you to stop eating the processed foods and snacks you enjoy is not helpful, you probably already know you should be doing it, and it seems like it's too hard to do so you don't bother. A great way to begin this process is to use a strategy of "fresh fibre first". I can't claim any credit for this as it was something I learned from Dr James Chestnut, but it's genius in its simplicity.

The first, and very important, thing is to not stop eating or drinking anything that currently brings you pleasure. Phew, what a relief! Stopping doing something that brings you pleasure is stressful and often unsustainable, and eventually you'll break and go back to it. What you must do, though, is eat something fresh and raw before any meal or snack. It could be a piece of fruit, a raw carrot or a little salad. If you never normally eat anything like this, try lots of different ones until you find one thing you especially like, then use that. It can't come from any package that has "ingredients" listed on the side and it must be fresh and raw. Why, you may ask? It's very stressful to say, "I love cake, but I can never eat cake again." However, eating your cake as you normally would but having an apple before it is much less stressful. You must always commit to eating it first, though. Don't fall into the habit of saying, "I'll eat it afterwards, I promise." Eating it first means it's much more likely to happen as, if you waited until the end of your meal, it would be too easy to say, "Oh, I'm full now. I'll do it next time." It also fills up your stomach a little bit with good, nourishing food and will help you to limit the amount of bad stuff you can put in. Whatever you eat after it, whatever the thing is that you can't give up, you can't take away the positive impact the fresh, raw food item will have had on your body.

If you did this for a year, eating a piece of raw, fresh food or a salad before every meal, at the end of the year, would you be healthier or sicker as a result? Of course, you'd be healthier and you wouldn't have given up a single cake, packet of crisps or burger. The real magic of this, though, is that after a short while of doing it consistently, you'll notice your cravings begin to shift and normalise. You'll view the food you thought you couldn't give up a little less favourably and your perception of it will change. You'll sense the positive impact that the fresh, raw food has and be tuned in to the negative impact of the other foods. Slowly, your eating choices will change in a gradual, stress-free way and your health will improve as a result.

The milk myth

A question I'm asked often when I explain that I don't eat dairy products is, "Where do you get your calcium from?" It's a reasonable question because we've been educated for years about the calcium content of milk and how calcium is essential for strong bones and teeth. But I always come back to the logical argument: where did your wild ancestors get their calcium from? Were they roaming around in packs, tracking female buffalo that just so happened to be nursing their young, and then chasing them down until they could catch them alive? Then, did they somehow manage to lead a half-tonne wild animal back to their camp and tie it up so they could milk it, risking being trampled on and gored the whole time? Or did they just hunt the animal for meat? What would they have done outside the breeding season when all the young buffalo had been weaned and their mothers were no longer producing milk? Did they all have osteoporosis at these times of the year?

The truth is, they never had osteoporosis. It's never been found in any fossil records. Your ancestors had extremely strong, dense bones, full of calcium and all the other minerals required. Perhaps they occasionally happened to hunt and kill an animal that was lactating, so I'm sure they would have drained the milk from it as an occasional lucky find, but it would never have formed a significant part of their diet and been their main source of dietary calcium. No, your ancestors got the bulk of their calcium from the same place the cows get it: from eating leafy green vegetables. It's just that cows eat grass and clover and you choose cabbage, spinach and kale.

If dairy cows are fed grain as their main food source without supplementation, they too become calcium deficient and so does their milk. Milk from healthy, naturally reared animals has quite a high calcium content, but that doesn't make it a good source of calcium for you. It's not in a form that's suitable for you to absorb and utilise and it comes with a lot of negative effects too, such as causing a high spike of insulin and also producing acidity in your bloodstream. Your blood should be around a neutral pH or slightly alkali, and if it becomes acidic (through a number of causes) your body has to try to neutralise it. It does this by actually dumping calcium into your blood, which alkalises it, bringing the pH down within a normal range. And where does it get this calcium from? Your bones! Your bones are the major storage areas for calcium in your body. Drinking dairy products causes your bones to be weakened as the calcium is taken from them to neutralise your acidic blood. It's the exact opposite to what you've been led to believe: milk contains calcium, we need calcium for strong bones, therefore milk is good for strong bones. But it really isn't.

Have you ever noticed the adverts for dairy products on TV? They never directly claim that eating their yoghurt will give you strong bones. They say it's a source of calcium and calcium is important for healthy bones and teeth. It's a subtle but important difference. In comparison, the calcium contained in green vegetables is in the perfect state for absorption and use by humans. And leafy greens also contain countless other vitamins and minerals beneficial to humans, unlike cows' milk.

Cows' milk is the perfect food to transform a weak young calf into a huge strong cow in the shortest possible time. It contains all the right proteins and hormones to support this transformation. It's not designed for humans and definitely not for adults. Your digestive system changes as you move from being a baby drinking only breast milk, to being weaned on to solid foods. You stop producing the enzyme lactase so you're no longer able to properly process and digest the main sugar found in milk called lactose.

And why cows' milk? It would make much more sense to drink breast milk as that's for humans, but the thought would probably revolt you. And would you drink pigs' milk or dogs' milk? I doubt it. We are the only species that's ever drunk the milk of another animal and continued to do so beyond infancy. Yet it's just not logical and, once you've been weaned, you have absolutely no nutritional need for any kind of milk. That also goes for products made from milk, such as cheese, butter and yoghurt. We've been convinced that dairy products are one of our essential food groups, all in the name of making money, but it's absolutely untrue. If you can tolerate them with no adverse effects, then by all means eat them very occasionally as I know they provide a lot of pleasure, but aim to avoid them whenever you can.

I'm certain that drinking milk is the wrong thing to do, but what should you drink? Again, look to your ancestors. Look to the people who shaped your genome. They drank what was available - which was simply water! It's what all other animals on the planet drink so why would the human animal need anything else? Fortunately for me, I've always enjoyed drinking water. When I'm thirsty, I want nothing other than a glass of cool, clear water and it's a natural craving that I'm certain is built into you too. It's just that there are so many drink products that are pushed upon us that are full of flavourings and sugars. They may taste pleasant but they can lead to your cravings being overridden. True, they obviously contain water, but there is also a huge burden of rubbish in there that your body has to deal with. They're either full of sugar that will be stored as fat, or artificial sweeteners that your body has no mechanism to deal with. They have chemical colours, flavourings and preservatives that can't possibly bring greater health.

Also, like me, I'm sure you've read that alcohol in moderation is good for you. There are often stories in the media claiming that two or three glasses of red wine per week are beneficial to you and that certain health indicators are improved as a result. I personally very much enjoy a glass of red wine with a meal or to relax at the end of a busy day, but I'm pragmatic about its benefits. When the studies have been done that claim these benefits, they're not comparing huge groups of perfectly healthy people, who lead the natural lives of humans, and saying that the ones who drink wine are healthier. They're comparing many average people who already lead a potentially less-than-healthy lifestyle, whose bodies have got a lot of crap to deal with on a daily basis.

Perhaps, and this is just a guess, if you're already leading a less-than-perfect lifestyle, the contents of red wine may help mitigate that to some degree and counteract the damage caused, giving you a slight advantage. Or maybe it's just the lowered stress levels and relaxation that alcohol can bring that helps. But, if we accept that true health is when every one of your 75 trillion cells is functioning exactly how it's meant to, abundant with all the nutrients your genes require to express health, how could adding wine make us more healthy? If you were a perfectly functioning human specimen operating at 100% health, adding wine couldn't give you more health. We didn't evolve drinking wine so there is no genetic requirement for it.

We are victims of our own success, becoming too clever. We've advanced to the point of civilisation where we are now but it's come at a great price. Before agriculture, we were taller, leaner and healthier, free from the modern plague of chronic illnesses. Our brains had grown because of our lifestyle and this led to greater intelligence and innovation, but it made us ignore the logic that got us to that point. Once we became farmers, we were able to grow large amounts of certain foods that provided us with a reliable source of calories and could always be used to feed us, but we were shorter on average and developed chronic illnesses that had never been seen before. As we've become more ingenious, we've decided that we know best and have forgotten that nature still applies to us as it does to all other animals.

We need to stop focusing on weight and directly linking it to illness. Being excessively overweight is definitely not a good idea, but just being fat isn't what moves you towards ill health. It's the things you've done to become fat that make you sicker. If you've eaten a diet rich in natural fruits and vegetables, and also healthy, naturally reared meats, but perhaps eaten a little too much, you'll store some of the excess as fat. However, your body will be properly nourished and able to thrive. If, on the other hand, you've eaten a diet high in the unnatural or incorrect things, such as processed foods, grains and sugars, you'll probably still put on weight but this time your body will literally be starved of nutrition and heading for illness. Being fat is not the cause of illness. It's the things that you ate on your way to becoming fat.

Some simple rules when eating out

If you cook all your meals at home from scratch, it can be relatively simple to ensure you're making good choices. You're in complete control of what you've got in your cupboards. However, what happens when you eat out? Sometimes it can be difficult to decide what is best. The salads section of the menu can be a good place to start, not because you're trying to lose weight but because you're trying to gain health! Salads are usually made up of a number of different raw, fresh plant foods with the addition of some protein, such as meat or fish. The plants are full of the vitamins and minerals required for health, which is great, but the protein is likely to be from an intensively farmed animal. This is because many restaurants are more focused on their profit margins than the nutrient composition, and therefore the "healthiness" of their meats, so consider that. Also, very often things like pasta, cous cous and other grain foods are included in the salads and these should ideally be kept to a minimum.

However, you may not want to eat a salad every time you're out. Sometimes it just won't do, especially on a cold winter's day. So, you could look for meals that don't contain pastry, batter or breadcrumbs, for instance. Avoid things that are deep fried if you can. If you opt for beef, unless it is specifically labelled as grass fed, assume that it was grain fed and, as such, contains a lot of the inflammatory omega 6 fats and very little omega 3. With chicken, you ideally want free range as it will have had the chance to scratch around in the dirt and eat bugs and grubs. It will have lived a more natural life in the process and have a more natural nutrient composition in its meat. Lamb is often a safe bet as sheep will generally only eat grass. If you can opt for vegetables or salad instead of fries, that could be a good choice too.

Now, you may be thinking I'm taking all the joy out of eating here! I understand that. I really enjoy food and eating out with friends and family. So, because the vast majority of the foods my family and I eat are prepared at home from fresh, real ingredients, when we eat out, we generally choose whatever we want. I love a great burger, some fresh bread or a creamy cheesy sauce! But I know these are not choices that bring health, only pleasure. And I don't know about you, but I enjoy pleasure! However, I also know that at other times, the majority of the foods I put into my body are providing the nutrients that my genome has evolved to require, and very few of the things that have been introduced in more recent years that it wasn't built to deal with.

CHAPTER 3

Alignment and Posture

As you know, I'm married to a chiropractor and have been immersed in the world of chiropractic and spinal health for most of my adult life. It's been my great fortune to listen to and meet some truly world-changing speakers over the past 20 years, who have devoted their lives to the search for true health. So it will come as little surprise that I consider posture and the correct alignment of your spine to be crucial to obtaining and maintaining a state of health and wellbeing.

Your spine carries out a number of tasks for you: it holds you upright and allows you to stand tall, rather than hunched over on all fours like your very distant ancestors; it has many other parts of your skeleton hanging off it, such as your ribs, your shoulders, your pelvis and your head; it allows incredible flexibility so you can bend and twist. But, most importantly for life and for health, it contains and protects your delicate central nervous system. All the other functions are just added bonuses in reality as, without the physical protection afforded by your spine to your central nervous system, life as you know it would be virtually impossible.

The only reason you can read this book is because billions and billions of signals are moving from your brain to your body, and then back from your body to your brain via your spinal cord. Without the spinal cord, your brain couldn't communicate with any part of your body. You wouldn't be able to hold this book or turn the pages, your eyes wouldn't convert the letters on the page to electrical impulses and send them to your brain, and walking and talking wouldn't exist, which are fairly obvious physical things. But you also wouldn't be breathing, your stomach wouldn't digest your last meal and your kidneys wouldn't be filtering waste products from your bloodstream. There are multiple things you can see and you're conscious of that rely on the nervous system, but there are many, many more that are happening all the time, 24 hours per day, unseen that you have no awareness of. In short, you owe your entire existence and life to your nervous system.

Because the spinal cord is so essential to life, you've evolved a very clever and intricate mechanism to protect it from external damage but, at the same time, give you the flexibility needed to be able to twist, bend, run and jump. This is, of course, your spine. Because I'm actually an electrical engineer, I think of the spine as a flexible conduit that protects the cabling within it from any physical external impact, while still allowing it to move to wherever it needs to go.

The spine is an arrangement of 24 moveable vertebrae that sit one on top of the other in a column. There is a hole through each vertebra towards the back where the spinal cord sits, and gaps between the vertebrae that enable your nerves to leave the spinal cord and reach every part of your body that requires a connection. The gaps are formed by the discs, which sit between the vertebrae, and these can be thought of as similar to a poached egg. They have a tough, rubbery outer ring like the egg white, and a softer, jelly-like centre similar to the egg yolk. There only needs to be a small amount of movement between each pair of vertebrae to allow the full range of bending and twisting that you would normally enjoy, as each small movement between the pairs when added together results in a large overall movement. So, the vertebrae tilt from side to side, front to back and rotate relative to each other, all the while allowing the delicate nerves to leave the spinal cord unhindered to carry the communication between your brain and body.

Nothing can happen in your body without a signal moving from your brain, down your spinal cord and out of the nerve root to your body part, and then a similar message going back from your body to the nerve and up the spinal cord back to your brain. Every time you move any muscles, take a breath or digest your breakfast, perfect signals to carry out these tasks leave your brain, travel along the correct part of your spinal cord, out along the nerve root and to the appropriate body part. Then perfect feedback signals from the body part take the same route back up to the correct part of the brain to keep it informed of progress. This is all happening at incredible speed without you being aware of any of it, whether you're running, sleeping or laughing. It truly is amazing.

If your very early ancestors hadn't evolved a protection mechanism for your spinal cord, it's extremely unlikely that life as we know it would exist. Your brain is protected by your skull, your heart by your ribcage and your nervous system by your spine.

You probably never give your spine a second thought as you can't see it and can't feel how well it's operating. It's just there at the back, allowing you to bend and twist. There could be slight physical changes occurring whereby the vertebrae are not quite gliding as well as they should due to muscle tightness or injury. Or, perhaps because of chronic inflammation in the body, small bits of bone are beginning to grow on the edges of the vertebrae but you have no idea they're there. Pressure on the nerves from these changes or an injury can cause nerve interference and change the signals flowing to and from your brain. It can speed them up; it can slow them down; it can also alter them so that they're not quite the same when they arrive at their destination, a bit like a game of Chinese whispers. Your brain is sending out a perfect message to your body, but it's not quite the same by the time it arrives. So the body part doesn't do exactly what your brain intended. Similarly, perhaps your body needs to alert your brain to something important and produces a perfect signal, but its path back to the brain is across a nerve that has interference, so the signal is slightly altered or arrives at the wrong time.

If this all sounds a little strange, think about when you've had something like pins and needles down your arm after sleeping awkwardly for a period of time perhaps, or your foot's gone to sleep after sitting in a funny position. This is nerve interference in action. The normal signal carrying your sense of touch that left your arm or foot was perfect initially, but as it travelled back to your brain it became slightly altered and the feeling your brain perceived was different. This is a simple one to grasp as you've probably experienced numbness or pins and needles many times in the past, but what would altered nerve signals to and from your liver feel like? Or your bowel or your stomach? You don't get a sense of touch from them, so you wouldn't feel numbness, for instance, but perhaps instead your food is not digested as well as it could be or maybe you experience Irritable Bowel Syndrome (IBS)?

It's only after a major injury, or an accumulation of many small injuries over many years, that we start to take notice. Often, the last resort is that your spine will alert you to a problem through pain. Suddenly, you become intensely aware of your spine even though you still can't see it. It could be that you've injured some of the hundreds of muscles and ligaments that hold it all together, or that there is pressure being applied to the nerves that leave the spinal cord through a misalignment in your spine, or there's just swelling in the muscles near to the nerve. Worst of all, it could be that the soft centre of a disc has begun to push through the outer ring and cause a bulge that presses directly on the nerve. This last one is often called a "slipped disc" but, in reality, it's a herniated disc or disc bulge, as your discs can't actually slip anywhere.

Pain is one of your body's methods of telling you to take action. It's usually the body's last resort as it's less easily ignored than the other earlier signs. Pain is your body shouting at you: "HELP ME! CHANGE SOMETHING NOW!" But what is the usual response to pain such as this? That's right, take a painkiller so that you no longer feel the pain. Your body is still shouting at you and the injury is still there but you can't hear it anymore. You feel better and are not aware of the pain, so you carry on moving and doing the things that led to the injury in the first place and the injury gets worse. Your body then shouts louder at you and the painkillers no longer numb your pain, so you take more. Or you take stronger and stronger ones. And the cycle goes on until no painkillers help and you find yourself at your GP's, who suggests surgery.

It's very similar to your smoke alarm at home. Imagine there is a fire in your house and the smoke alarm goes off. It's beeping and screaming at you and it's very annoying. You can't hear the TV over it; won't someone please stop that noise? But rather than investigate and then put out the fire, you cover up the smoke alarm or just take out the battery. The annoying beeping has stopped and you can carry on watching your favourite programme, but the fire is still burning. Obviously not a good idea!

It makes more sense to find the source of the fire, or the source of the pain, and remove it. It makes even more sense to prevent the fire occurring in the first place by checking for potential sources of ignition and keeping your house free of combustibles. Or, in the case of pain, checking the movement and position of your spine and correcting any smaller issues before they grow larger. This is what chiropractors are trained to do.

Vertebrae in your spine that are not moving as they should be or that are not in their correct positions are said to be dysfunctional. Your chiropractor will often refer to these dysfunctional areas as subluxations. Chiropractors are the only people trained to locate, analyse and remove subluxations of the spine, and that forms the main focus of their care. Subluxations are often located through manually feeling along your spine, checking for movement between the vertebrae and making sure they're in their proper position. Sometimes these areas are also measured or confirmed using a scanner or other device. Often, severely subluxated areas cause pain and discomfort nearby or, in many cases, pain, numbness or pins and needles in the part of the body that the affected nerve is connected to. This is because of altered nerve signals and interference. Frequently, other areas of your body are also affected but you either can't feel the difference or don't realise that the internal symptoms you have are caused by the interference.

Betty's story

In their final year of study, student chiropractors work in the college clinic caring for real patients. One of my wife Julia's patients, when she was working in the college clinic, was a lady in her late sixties. Betty came to the clinic because of low back pain that had improved really well after just a few visits. In college, the students are only allowed to adjust their patients (which is the term used by a chiropractor when they manipulate the joints) in the areas that they've been told are painful but, after a few weeks, Betty happened to mention in conversation that she took about 12 to 14 antacids every day plus a whole bottle of Gaviscon per week. To say she had indigestion was definitely an understatement!

Because of some reading she had done previously as part of her studies, Julia had become aware that spinal problems can often influence organs in the body because of the nerve interference that subluxations can cause. Without her tutors knowing, Julia asked Betty if she'd mind if she tried to help her indigestion. Of course, Betty was more than happy to say yes following Julia's great results with her back pain. Julia checked T6, which is the level of the spine where the nerves to the stomach exit, and found it to be subluxated. She adjusted it and thought little more about it, until Betty came back the following week and reported that her symptoms had reduced so much that she'd dropped down to taking just three half tablets per day! This was the first time Julia realised that chiropractic could help many more things than just back pain and headaches.

Richard's story

Richard was a 36-year-old mechanic. He had suffered with back pain for many years, pain he assumed was caused by his job. He visited the clinic after being recommended by his wife, who had had great results with her conditions.

Julia checked Richard for subluxations and found them at the areas that were painful but also at other levels of the spine. She adjusted him at all the levels she'd found. Richard felt his pain improve immediately and was happy as he left that day.

Later that week when he came for his next adjustment, he asked Julia, "What did you do to me last time?" She was a little taken aback but he then explained that he rarely felt hungry, only ate at home because his wife forced him to and survived on around 40 cups of sweet tea every day (each one taken with four spoonfuls of sugar). It had been this way for as long as he could remember but the evening after his first visit, his stomach rumbled! Richard and his wife were sitting together on the sofa and it took them both by surprise as it had never happened before. Richard felt hungry!

Julia repeated what she'd told him at his previous visit, about how the nervous system controls everything and any interference to it can lead to a wide variety of symptoms, only one of which is pain. The subluxation she'd found and adjusted at T6 was probably the reason for his previous lack of hunger pangs.

It's not uncommon to get some large, immediate results following an adjustment but you're more likely to get smaller incremental ones that build up over time. However, everyone is different. Richard jokes that he now has the inconvenience of having to take a packed lunch to work with him otherwise he gets hungry! His health has improved in so many ways because his nervous system is now free of interference and his body is properly nourished.

The importance of posture

The part of your spine with the greatest amount of movement and flexibility is your neck. Your cervical spine, as it's known, needs to allow your head to look left and right, up and down and also tilt to the sides. Coupled with supporting the weight of your head, which in an average adult is around 10lbs, your neck is an amazing structure. It also houses and protects the uppermost part of your spinal cord just after it leaves your brain and skull. Every signal that leaves the brain to travel down the spinal cord has to pass through this connection between the spine and the skull at the first cervical vertebra, C1, or atlas as it's known. So problems with the cervical spine can affect many areas of the body.

When a chiropractor checks your posture, one thing he or she is looking for is anterior head carriage or, in plain English, if your head is further forward than it should be. Your head should sit nicely on top of your neck so that it takes very little effort to keep this 10lb weight in the air. If it's jutting forward, however, because of gravity it will actually appear heavier to your body and will take more energy and effort to keep it up. This eventually shortens the muscles at the front of the neck and overuses and weakens the muscles at the back, which can lead to the loss of range of motion, meaning you'll have a stiff neck and can't move it how you used to be able to. The result can often be headaches and the appearance of a hunched back as your head sits further and further forward and your shoulders become more and more rounded over time.

However, you can't see the worst aspect of anterior head carriage unless you look at an MRI of the spinal cord. It causes the spinal cord to be stretched slightly and held under constant tension, which has the capacity to interfere with all the signals flowing up and down between your brain and body. This can have devastating effects on your health and the function of your body - which I realise can sound a little hard to swallow, but there are many research papers that link the degree of anterior head carriage with an increase in something termed "all cause mortality". In a paper titled *Hyperkyphotic Posture Predicts Mortality in Older Community-dwelling Men and Women: A Prospective Study*, the researchers found a direct link between how forward a person's head was and how likely they were to die prematurely from any cause! Those with the characteristic rounded-shoulder or hunched-back posture had a 1.44 greater chance of dying prematurely when compared to the people with more normal posture. That's incredible and shows just how important posture is to your health and wellbeing. It's estimated that only around 10% of the individual fibres that make up the spinal cord and nerves carry signals that relate to pain and feeling, so if a nerve is being pinched enough to cause pain, what else is being altered that you're not aware of?

Your curves

When viewed from the side, your spine should have three distinct curves that together form a smooth, flowing S shape. The three curves relate to the cervical spine, or neck, the thoracic spine, or mid back, and the lumbar spine, or low back. This shape gives the spine a lot of its cushioning and spring and allows you to walk, run and jump without jolting and jarring the joints of your spine with every step. Imagine if you didn't have the curves and your spine was a totally straight column of bones, one on top of the other. You would still have some shock absorption from the discs but there would be many more jolts and shocks going through your spine without the curves to give you the bounce. Your discs would experience a greater force through them with every step you took, or each time you lifted a heavy load, and this would inevitably lead to premature aging and greater risk of disc bulges and prolapsed discs. The discs themselves have a relatively poor blood supply and fluid within them is gradually squeezed out during your day because of gravity and the loads they are subjected to. They are then able to reabsorb nutrient-rich fluid overnight while you lie in your bed. You're actually two to three centimetres taller in the morning than you are at the end of a hard day, because all your discs have been pumped back up!

At the rear of your vertebrae there are a pair of facet joints at each vertebral level that provide stability to your spine, allowing the bones to move and glide over one another without them coming apart. Synovial fluid is present within your facet joints and acts as a lubricant to allow the bones to glide over one another easily. If pairs of vertebrae are not moving because of a long-standing injury, the joints can begin to dehydrate and become stiff. Dehydrated, stiff joints become inflamed, leading to unpleasant and painful symptoms. Movement of the joint is what stimulates the production of fluid and allows it to get where it is needed. I liken it to a rusty gate hinge: to get oil into the hinge and keep it moving easily, you must first squirt oil around the moving parts. But only after you've opened and closed the gate several times to work the hinge does the oil actually get drawn into where it needs to be. Your body can produce the fluid but it only gets where it needs to be with movement.

Poor posture doesn't just feel bad and cause painful symptoms. It also looks bad! Aesthetically speaking, you already know this. If you see someone who is hunched over with very rounded shoulders, or who has a pronounced forward head carriage, they just don't look good. They don't look healthy and will appear shorter and older than they actually are. Similarly, if a person with excellent posture enters a room, they are generally eye catching and look positive and confident. They'll appear younger, vibrant and more "alive"! This can be very important for some people in their work life, for instance if they work in sales where they need to appear confident or knowledgeable, or have to stand in front of a group to give a presentation.

Good posture can also affect your mood and alertness. The next time you find yourself feeling a little low or flat, check your posture. If you're slouched or have rounded shoulders, make a conscious effort to improve your posture for a few minutes and feel the effect for yourself.

There's a brilliant example of this on the TED.com website in a talk given by Amy Cuddy (https://www.ted.com/talks/amy_cuddy_your_body_language_shapes_who_you_are), where she describes the research she's carried out into the physiological effects of posture on the body. By adopting an upright, "powerful" pose for just a couple of minutes, her subjects significantly increased their testosterone levels, giving a feeling of more confidence, and lowered their levels of the stress hormone cortisol, making them more relaxed. I would highly recommend you find her presentation and watch it.

The six Ss

Posture affects, and is affected by, six main areas. These are what I call the six Ss: Standing; Sitting; Squatting; Slobbing; Sleeping; and finally Screens.

Standing

When in a neutral position and viewed from the side, your ear, shoulder, hip, back of the knee and ankle should all form a straight line. The person in figure 1 shows this, but notice the changes in the relative positions in figure 2.

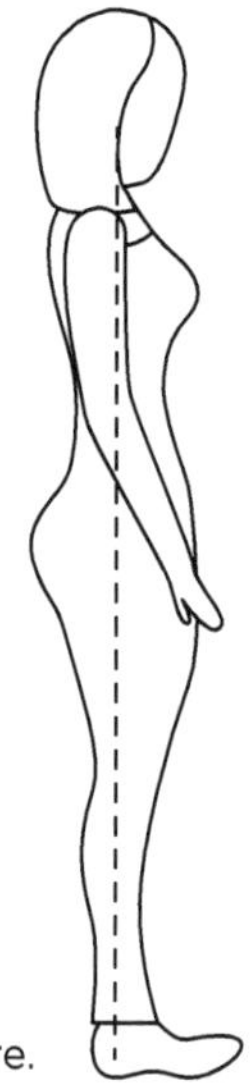

Figure 1 : Good posture.

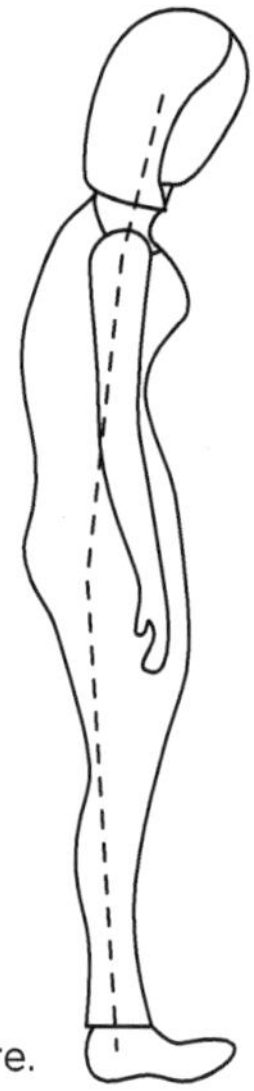

Figure 2: Poor posture.

The shoulders are rolled forward along with the head, and the spine has lost its natural S curve. You can't see it but the spinal cord will be under tension in the neck and we now know that hormonal levels are altered too as a result. Often the cause of this posture is tight pectoral muscles across your chest, coupled with weakened muscles across your shoulders and upper back. There is a fairly simple exercise to correct this, which, if repeated twice a day for a month, will make dramatic changes to your posture. It's called the YWTL.

YWTL

Preparation - Hold your arms above your head in a Y position with locked elbows as shown in figure 3. Make sure your thumbs are pointing behind you and stand as tall as you can. Tuck your chin in and don't allow your back to arch or tummy to stick out.

Take a deep breath in and fill your lungs as much as you can. Then, whilst breathing out, pull your shoulder blades close together for a count of three. Keep the tension on your shoulder blades and take another deep breath. Don't lose the tension while inhaling and make sure to keep your chin tucked back. Then, when you breathe out,

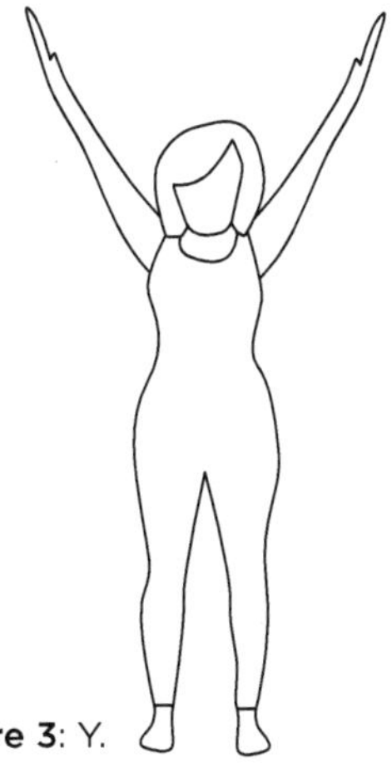

Figure 3: Y.

squeeze your shoulder blades together again. Repeat this one more time for a total count of three. Think of each breath out as a ratchet, not allowing your shoulder blades to relax but making them tighter each time. On the final breath out, you'll really feel the pull!

Now repeat it all again with your arms in the W, T and L positions shown in figures 4, 5 and 6 respectively.

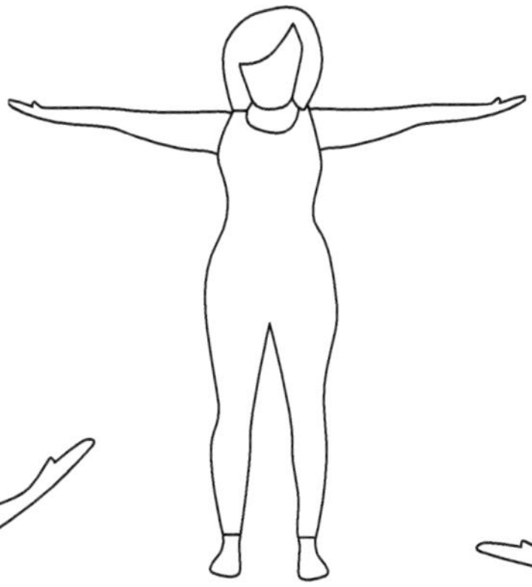

Figure 5: T.

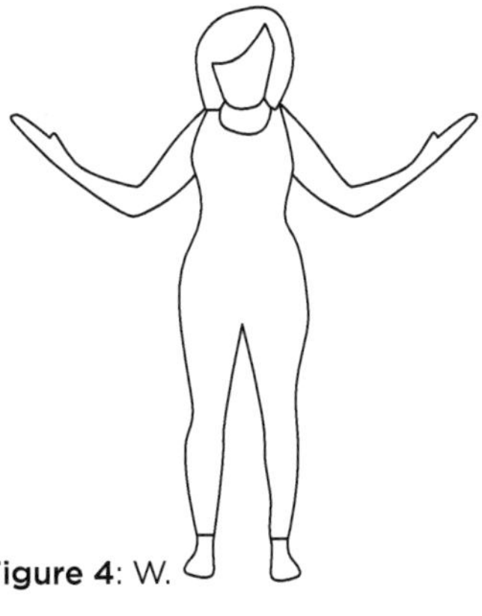

Figure 4: W.

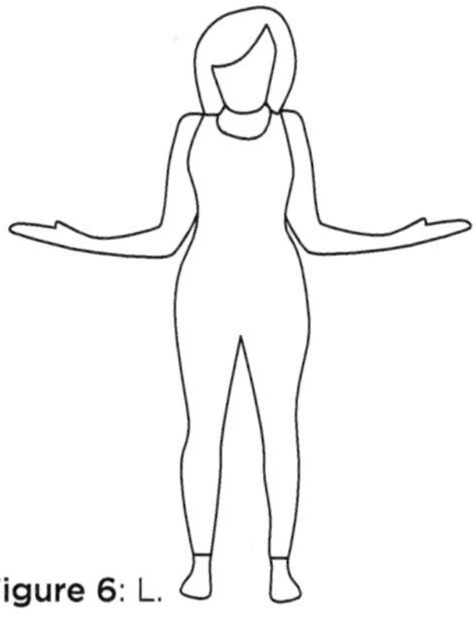

Figure 6: L.

Each position changes the orientation of the muscles in your upper back and chest, allowing different levels to be targeted. This increases the overall strength of the muscles across your upper back, which helps to hold your head up, while stretching out the tight muscles across your chest that are trying to pull your head forward.

Completing this exercise once or twice per day for a month will make a big improvement to your posture and upper body strength, not to mention lowering your risk of many other conditions.

Another simple strategy is to make sure you are conscious of your posture as often as possible and actively correct it whenever you notice that it's not good, for instance, when driving or standing in a queue.

Sitting

Many of us now spend an awfully long time sitting down in our everyday lives. This can be working at a desk, commuting to work or just relaxing. However, at no point in our evolution did we sit for long periods of time. Our bodies are not adapted for it and it's thought to be responsible for many musculoskeletal conditions that people seek help for. Your ancestors will have only occasionally sat and would have been much more likely to squat when relaxing or they were working on something at low level. It's what wild humans currently do and, if you've ever noticed babies once they start to walk, they frequently squat down rather than sit on the floor, if left to their own devices.

Bad sitting practices cause a lot of problems in your spine and are responsible for many of the conditions that patients initially seek our care for help with. In our modern society, it's impossible to avoid sitting, but to minimise the impact when seated, your hips should be higher than your knees. If your chair won't allow this, opt for a seat wedge to help. If you sit at a desk, adjust the seat height so that your elbows are slightly higher than your wrists, especially when using a keyboard. Very supportive, or so-called ergonomic, chairs are not always the best option, as they tend to encourage slouching or leaning back into the seat back. It's better to adopt some form of active sitting, if possible, using a seat that's unstable to a degree with little support.

In our clinic, everyone uses stools like this called "swoppers" that are designed to mimic sitting on a gym ball - or you could just use a gym ball if you have the space! The reason these are better is that, because of the lack of support and the instability, they encourage you to use the core muscles around your abdomen and lower back to keep yourself upright. When we first introduced them behind the reception desk, everyone complained for the first few days that they ached as if they'd just started going to the gym and been doing sit-ups! However, by the end of the week they were fine and now know they get a mini core workout whilst sitting down!

Whatever you choose to sit on, make time to get up occasionally and twist, stretch and bend to keep your spine flexible.

Squatting

As already stated, in many parts of the world, squatting down with your feet flat on the floor is a very normal alternative to sitting. However, in western cultures we seem to have lost this ability and most people can't achieve it without falling backwards, or they have to balance on the balls of their feet. Young children do it instinctively but as they grow and reduce their flexibility through poor habits, they lose the ability.

It's a great way to stretch and strengthen your lower back and thighs. Start by squatting as low as you can whilst keeping your feet flat on the floor, as shown in figure 7.

Figure 7: Squat.

Don't let you heels lift at all but steady yourself against a chair or wall until you get the hang of it. Hold the squat for a few seconds and then stand again. You may find it helps initially to have your feet wider apart and pointing at a "ten to two" position. Repeat this a number of times over a month and watch as you're able to get lower and lower, until eventually you can hold the squat comfortably at the very bottom for as long as you want. This could be used as a simple exercise in your stretch breaks during periods of prolonged sitting.

Slobbing

Most people are probably guilty of this occasionally, especially when relaxing at the end of a long day. Your body lies almost parallel with the sofa and your head is propped up against the back cushion. It feels relaxing to slouch into a comfy chair sometimes and I know I'm guilty of it. However, it stretches and weakens the muscles at the back of your neck and can encourage those at the front to tighten, leading to poor posture when not slouched. It also stretches your spinal cord and restricts the airways, hampering your breathing. Sitting or even falling asleep in a slouched position for long periods can lead to neck stiffness, pain and headaches. Doing the YWTL exercise can help repair this damage. However, try to avoid slobbing if possible.

Sleeping

One of the most common questions a chiropractor is asked is: "Should I have a hard or soft mattress?" There is unfortunately no right or wrong answer. It's a very individual thing based on a number of factors. Ideally, you should sleep on your side or possibly your back, but never on your front. Sleeping on your front can cause a lot of problems in your neck as it's twisted round for long periods of time. It also restricts your breathing as you have to lift your torso as your chest expands with every breath. When lying on your side, your spine should be relatively straight when viewed from the back. This is where the individuality comes in, because if you have very broad shoulders, for instance, you may need a softer mattress to allow the shoulder you're lying on to sink further in and keep the rest of your spine straight.

Similarly, you'll need to find a suitable pillow to keep your head supported and your spine in line, so it's really a combination of the pillow, mattress and your body shape that will determine what's best for you.

When Julia and I buy a new mattress, we try lots of them out in the shop and check each other's spines for alignment until we find one that's right. If the sales assistant in the shop doesn't seem to want you to do this, I would take your business elsewhere to someone more helpful, as poorly chosen mattresses and pillows can have a massive effect on the health of your spine and nervous system. After all, you spend around a third of your life in bed, so choose wisely.

Screens

This is a more recent phenomenon and is having a huge impact on posture and spinal health. Many of us spend hours and hours in front of screens of one type or another, from your computer at work to your laptop, and from tablets to smart phones. I've already covered good sitting at a computer screen on a desk but ideally, if you can, try to stand when using them. If you can afford it, buy a standing desk or, in the meantime, use some suitable height boxes on your desk, perhaps with a piece of plywood or similar on top. Then your screen, mouse and keyboard can sit on this. If using a laptop, try not to sit for long periods with it actually on your lap! You'll find you're looking down an awful lot, which will likely lead to headaches and stiffness. This also goes for iPads, tablets and smart phones. There is actually a recognised condition now called "text neck" that is caused by looking down at a hand-held screen for long periods of time. This, of course, leads to anterior head carriage and all the other knock-on effects already described.

Because I'm passionate about chiropractic and the enormous benefits it can bring to your life, I'm obviously biased. For many years, the chiropractic profession has been ridiculed and denounced as quackery by many from medical backgrounds, even though chiropractors see amazing transformations in health occur every day. However, there is a huge body of properly executed scientific research that directly links the function of your spine and nervous system to your overall health and longevity. Much of it is not written by chiropractors but by people investigating human physiology and health. It confirms the results that have been obtained by chiropractors for over 100 years. If you want to be the best you can be, you can't ignore the function of your spine.

CHAPTER 4

Thoughts

Most people, if asked, would not consider thoughts to be that important in terms of health. I mean, how could they be? They're just patterns of electrical impulses flying around countless brain cells in your head. The majority of medical science has considered the human body to be nothing more than a biomechanical machine as long as medicine has existed as a profession; just like any other machine, you put in fuel and the things it needs to stay in good repair, and you direct it to do whatever you want to do – move around, run, jump, speak etc. Talk of a mind-body connection would usually invite ridicule and eye rolling and I used to be no different. Coming from an engineering background as I did, I always thought in physical, visible and tangible ways. If you can't see it or pick it up, it can't be real. I couldn't really understand what the term "mind" meant anyway and I assumed it was just another word for brain. As I've become exposed to some different viewpoints and tried to be more open to new ideas, I've realised that the mind is so incredibly important that to ignore and dismiss it is nonsensical, and can render any other health interventions you apply to be almost pointless.

Now I think of the brain as the group of 100 billion nerve cells and the 100 trillion electrical connections between them that make up the physical organ that lives in your head; the thing you could actually pick up. And I think of the mind as the function and processing that physical thing carries out on your behalf while you are alive. Your brain is tangible but your mind is not.

However, whatever your personal thoughts on this distinction, you can't ignore the fact that the body is almost entirely under the control of the mind. The physical thing you see in the mirror is controlled by the beautifully orchestrated torrent of electrical activity that flows around and in and out of your brain under the direction of your mind, 24 hours per day, over your entire life. From the biggest, most powerful muscles moving in your body, to the tiniest, almost undetectable changes in hormone secretion, your mind controls them all and usually without you ever being conscious of it.

So, because anything physical that happens in your body begins as an electrical impulse in your brain under the direction of your mind, it's ridiculous to assume that thoughts you consciously (or unconsciously) create can't affect the body. Conversely, because the body is constantly feeding back signals to the brain via its network of 45 miles of nerves, and then altering its processing accordingly, it's incorrect to say that the brain isn't influenced by the body. This for me is the mind-body connection: a permanent, highly complex, two-way conversation between your physical, tangible body and your invisible, intangible mind.

Thinking about happy memories from your past, or things you enjoy and that make you happy, will cause your mind to signal happy hormones, such as dopamine and serotonin, to be released. These will course throughout your entire body leading to a feeling of increased wellbeing. On the other hand, bringing stressful thoughts to mind and worrying about what could happen will create an avalanche of stress hormones, such as cortisol and adrenalin, that signal the body to make physical changes in readiness for an attack of some nature; an attack that in all likelihood is never going to happen.

I'm sure you can remember waking from a bad dream at some point and experiencing those few moments of anxiety and fear, before your conscious mind begins to realise that it's not real; the enormous, snarling lioness isn't in your bedroom about to pounce on you, even though you could hear her growling and feel her breath on your skin. Your heart is beating rapidly, you're breathing heavily and, if you could measure your hormone levels at that point, they would be very similar to where they would be had you actually been running for your life on the African plains. Your body would be physically getting ready to run from the danger if possible, or stand and fight if that was your best option. Adrenalin would be elevated to make your heart beat faster and your breathing would be heavier and deeper to ensure as much oxygenated blood got to your muscles as possible. Your senses would be heightened so that you could have the best possible chance of survival in that situation, and your blood chemistry would have changed almost instantly to get ready for the possible healing that was going to be needed, so clotting agents and our old friend cholesterol would be elevated.

Boom boom boom, your heart is pounding; you're acutely aware of the slightest movement in your surroundings, even though your bedroom is in near total darkness. Every little noise, from the creaks of your floorboards to the knocking of your central heating pipes, is really loud. Your head and eyes are flicking around trying to spot where the threat is coming from.

But it's not real. There's nothing physical or tangible about it. Your mind has altered your body's physical state, or your physiology, to give you the best chance of escaping from the lioness. And just take a second or two to feel your heartbeat now, because writing this last paragraph made my heart beat faster! I wonder if reading it did the same to you? Where's the lioness? In your mind! Thankfully, the opposite is also true for pleasurable thoughts and feeling happy.

So the mind alters the body but it works in the opposite direction too. Physical actions that you direct your body to do can alter your brain chemistry. Smiling, even if you're not feeling particularly happy, causes your mind to release the same hormones to elevate your mood as if you were already happy, so your mood improves. Do it now, give it a go. Look up from the book and smile as widely as you can. Hold it for a few seconds and feel the positive changes in your mood. Endorphins in your body will rise while your stress hormones, such as cortisol, will lower. Chemical changes will occur driven by the physical position you've put your body into.

In the previous chapter, I mentioned a TED talk by Amy Cuddy about the hormonal changes that occur in your body just by adopting a powerful physical pose. You move yourself into position and the body directs the mind to release the associated hormones. If you didn't watch the video whilst reading the last chapter, I urge you to do so now. Cuddy isn't some wacko, out-there, new-age hippy, if that's what you're thinking. She's a highly respected and well-known researcher.

So thoughts – that is, invisible electrical impulses in your mind – become physical changes in your body via altered blood chemistry and hormone levels. Conversely, the physical positions you direct your body to adopt make actual changes in your mind. In very simple terms, this is the mind–body connection. So why are we not exploiting this knowledge to create positive changes in our state of health? The truth is, many people are doing so, from athletes to psychologists, from life coaches to researchers, and all with positive outcomes.

Some ground-breaking research by Dr Richard Suinn and his team at Colorado State University involved two groups of athletes in their study. Both groups trained normally as they had been doing but the second group was also directed to spend time mentally picturing themselves competing in the event, running the perfect race and performing better than they had ever done. The outcome was remarkable: the athletes who visualised themselves performing well made much greater improvements in their fitness, strength and personal-best times than the group who only trained physically. That's a powerful advantage all of us could be exploiting if we knew about it. It doesn't only have to be used for athletics. You could use it to enhance performance in any activity you carry out that requires an element of physical skill or hand-eye coordination.

In his book *When the Body Says No* (Vermilion, 2019), Dr Gabor Matte describes the phenomenal changes that the mind can illicit over the body, in particular the effect that mental or psychological trauma in a person's formative years can have on their physical wellbeing in later life. In one study, psychologists interviewed patients who had been admitted to hospital for a breast biopsy. The patients involved had either found a lump on their breast through physical examination or something had been spotted on a mammogram, and so were having the biopsy to determine if the lump was actually cancerous or not. Through interview questions alone, the researchers uncovered traumatic events in the childhoods of the patients, noted certain character traits, and were able to predict the presence of cancer in 94% of cases.

In a similar German study, 40 women with breast cancer were interviewed along with 40 healthy women of similar age, general health status and lifestyle. The researchers did not know the health status of the 80 women. Again, on psychological grounds only, the researchers were 96% successful in picking out the women who actually had cancer.

There are many other similar studies of patients with a variety of types of cancers that all have a very high accuracy. Yes, that is as incredible as it sounds: psychological abuse leading to certain character traits can influence the likelihood of developing cancer in later life, and answering a few simple questions about the nature of the abuse can predict the risk!

This is a relatively new topic in health and is frequently dismissed as non-scientific by those in the general medical field because it doesn't involve taking a pill or cutting out a body part. However, if you'd like to learn more, then read a book by Bruce Lipton PhD called *The Biology of Belief* (Hay House UK, 2015). In it, Lipton describes in detail, at a cellular and DNA level, the mind-body connection and why we can't assume the two things are separate.

The placebo effect is real

I'm sure you've heard of the placebo effect. It's the term given to the phenomenon of spontaneous healing that occurs in a person just because they believe they are going to get better. People can have had a condition for any period of time with no improvement, but once they are given a "magic pill", the condition begins to heal and they regain their health. The troubling thing for medicine is that this magic pill can often contain nothing active at all and is frequently just sugar or some other non-therapeutic substance.

When a new drug is being tested in a clinical trial, this is the basis of deciding whether it has any merit or not. It is compared to a placebo - that is, a false, pretend, inactive pill, and very often the drug performs no better or even worse than the placebo. How can this be? It's because of the mind-body connection. The patient believes so strongly that they are going to start healing and become well that their body actually does what is required for that to happen. The secret cure to their ills was within them all along, they just didn't know how to tap into it. Only once they truly believed that they were going to get well did the healing start.

The gold standard for testing a new drug's efficacy is what is known as a "double blind randomised placebo controlled trial". In this type of trial, there are two groups of patients, with one group getting the real drug and the other getting the fake drug. It's randomised because the people in each group are selected at random, and it's double blind because neither the patients nor the person administering the pills know who's in which group. This removes the potential for any outside factors to influence the results. Often both sets of people experience improvements in their conditions, but those getting the real drug have to be significantly more improved than the placebo group for the drug to be classed as effective.

This is built into our DNA but we enhance and emphasise it from a young age. How many times when you were a child did you hurt yourself, only to have your mum "kiss it better"? You believed that mum had magic kisses and that your bump would now begin to heal. This is often reinforced in our early years because, whenever we are ill or injured, we always go to see the doctor. We are conditioned to believe that we'll heal once we've stepped foot into the surgery and had our one-to-one consultation, even if we're just told to "come back in a week if it's no better". Whether we're given a prescription or not, the simple act of visiting the doctor often triggers our built-in healing process because we've now taken some action.

You may feel this kind of result means that, in reality, the patient wasn't really ill at all. They weren't ill, got a sugar pill instead of a drug and began to feel better through some psychological process. But, remarkably, the placebo effect is present in surgical procedures too! In the 2002 study titled "A controlled trial of Arthroscopic Surgery for Osteoarthritis of the Knee" by Bruce Moseley et al, two groups of people with similar knee complaints all got significant improvement in their pain and mobility scores following a surgical procedure. The interesting fact is, one of the two groups of patients was given anaesthetic, prepped for surgery and then opened up using a scalpel but with nothing else being done, other than obviously stitching of the incision.

Much to the surgeon's surprise, the people who had had the pretend surgery got similar, and often better, immediate and long-term results to the patients who had had the full surgical procedure! How can that be? It's because they truly believed that the condition they had been suffering from for many months or years was now going to be fixed because of the surgery. As far as they were concerned, they were sure they'd been through the full surgical procedure as no one had told them anything different. They even had the scars, stitches and post-surgery soreness to confirm it! Amazingly, their improvements were purely derived from their minds' ability to trigger healing in their bodies.

So, if the simple action of taking a sugar pill or experiencing a sham surgical procedure but truly believing, or even *knowing*, that it is going to help you is all it takes, can you see the incredible power within your mind to influence your body? And why could it be that the real drug or surgery performs worse than the fake one in many cases? If just taking a pill is enough to trigger the placebo effect, why don't both groups see similar improvements? My belief is that it's because your body now has to process the toxic drug or recover from the real surgery, and this takes an extra toll on your capacity to heal.

Of course, there could be many illnesses that you don't have the built-in capacity to heal from without some intervention, and I'm not for one minute declaring that you should abandon any medical help if it's required. My reasons for writing this chapter are to help you see the incredible power of the mind, your thoughts, attitude and outlook, and how you can benefit from them every day, not only when you're ill.

Imagine if you lived your life with positivity and hope all the time, with joy and gratitude occupying your mind and no negative thoughts. If you made real changes to your lifestyle, such as a natural diet, great posture, appropriate exercise and all the other areas covered in this book, and you felt great about that and *knew* it was going to have a massive, positive impact on your health, how much more benefit would you get from the knowing and certainty that you would avoid chronic lifestyle-related illness? You can harness the power of the placebo effect every day, but don't think of it as placebo. Just think of it as the incredible power of your mind to influence your body.

In my limited experience of people with chronic illnesses, I've seen two different kinds of progression. There are those who are given a diagnosis of, say, cancer, and become depressed and negative. They have a feeling of hopelessness and they give up. Then there are those who are given the same diagnosis but say to themselves, "Right, this isn't going to get me whatever you say. I'm going to beat it." The ones who have the fighting spirit seem to survive longer and have a greater chance of remission than the ones who just give up.

How many times have you heard about the tragic case of the person who was given a diagnosis and died a week later? Probably many times, unfortunately. But then there are those who live for many years more than their specialist told them they would and go on to beat their illness. This is a difficult thing to measure or to claim any proof for, but I'm certain that your attitude at this tough time has a huge impact on the outcome.

Take control of your monkey mind

So, how can you control the thoughts in your head? If you're anything like me, you probably feel as though you have hundreds of thoughts flashing through your mind from one minute to the next, and can quite easily find yourself thinking about obscure things that seem totally unrelated. A book I read many years ago on meditation likened this kind of thought process to a small monkey tied to a stake in the ground. Picture the frantic jumping and wriggling of the monkey as it tries to escape the rope, flicking and twitching one way and then the other. This image has always stayed with me and I now become aware of it especially when under states of intense mental pressure or stress.

I began to read about meditation and mindfulness and found that there is a huge array of different techniques you can employ to calm your monkey mind and have it sitting there contentedly next to the stake, with a slack rope, in peace. I was fortunate enough to attend a meditation course as a birthday gift a few years back and meditation is something I try to practise most days.

For you, the term "meditation" might seem a bit weird and conjure up images of a room full of people in white robes, all sitting cross-legged and saying, "Om" in unison. And that could be true. But meditation, or mindfulness, can take many forms and be done at any time without anyone ever knowing what you're doing.

When your monkey mind is left to its own devices, it is generally flipping from thoughts about the past to worries about the future. That is, things that have already happened and can't be changed, and other things that have not yet happened or might never happen. Allowing these kinds of thoughts to fill your brain for long periods of time is pointless, exhausting and will probably have a negative impact on your mood. You can't do anything about them so why devote huge amounts of your mind's resources to them?

Mindfulness

Mindfulness is simply the action of being in the moment - that is, only focusing on and thinking about what is happening right now. No thoughts of last year, yesterday or even ten minutes ago but right now. Not worrying about what you need to do tomorrow or what will happen if you don't do it, or any other "what ifs". Just now. Your mind will benefit from you being mindful for just a few minutes at a time and, if you can repeat it several times a day, the effect will be multiplied.

You could try being mindful whilst doing the ordinary, mundane tasks of the day, such as brushing your teeth or making a cup of tea. When brushing your teeth, for instance, don't allow yourself to think about anything else other than the simple action of moving your toothbrush in and out, up and down. In a slow, purposeful manner, clean your teeth and focus on how the toothpaste feels and tastes as it moves around your mouth. Notice the feeling of the brush on your gums, the sounds that it makes as it moves over your teeth, and where your tongue is. Be aware of the number of brush strokes you've used on each section of your mouth; upper left, upper right, upper front etc. Be entirely in the moment, thinking about nothing other than what you are doing right now. If you find yourself drifting off to worry about yesterday, or next week, just come back to the feelings now. Try doing this with your eyes closed to heighten the awareness of the sensations or sounds. Once you become better at it, it will perhaps take you two minutes to clean your teeth, during which time your monkey will be sitting patiently on the ground, calmly waiting for you to finish.

Mindful eating is also a great way to calm your mind, although this can be easier on your own initially. Notice the colours of the foods on your plate and how the food is laid out. Notice the aroma. Eat more slowly than you would normally and savour every bite, being aware of the temperatures, textures and tastes as you chew. How does the food sound as you bite, crunch or chew and then swallow? Again, if you notice that your mind wanders somewhere else, come back to your food and what you'll eat next. It will take a little longer to eat your meal, but a positive side effect of this is you'll probably eat less and notice the "full" signal your stomach sends to your brain before you overeat. Often those who are overweight may lose weight as a result of mindful eating, which can be a welcome bonus.

Whatever you become mindful at, your brain will have had a rest and the effects of this are cumulative. The more you do it - the more tasks or activities you can do consciously - the more you'll feel the positive effects of reduced emotional stress and increased peace.

Meditation

There are numerous different meditation techniques you can practise. Some involve silence and removal of any stimulation;

some require you to make specific audible sounds or think about a word; others involve listening to a recording that takes you on a mental journey. Listening to someone, what is often termed a "guided meditation", can be a good place to start. There are numerous free guided meditations available on YouTube if you'd like to try them out. There are also smartphone apps available, such as "Headspace".

You can sit in silence and become mindful of your breathing, not thinking about anything else other than the sensations as you breathe in and out; how the air feels rushing through your nose or mouth; how your chest rises and falls with each breath and the sounds the air makes.

The birthday gift I mentioned earlier in this chapter was a two-day transcendental meditation course given to me a few years back. This is a meditation that involves the repeated thought of an apparently meaningless two-syllable word whilst sitting in silence. The word is given to you by the teacher and is known as your mantra. I learnt a great deal from the course and, while my meditation has evolved slightly from the original course content, I don't think this matters because I still get benefit from it and give my mind an opportunity to switch off for 20 minutes every day.

In simple terms, I sit in an upright position with my back supported. I wait for 30 seconds and allow myself to relax and sink into the chair, feeling it support me. For 20 minutes, I then repeat my mantra word in my head in silence, in groups of three as I exhale. So the pattern becomes: inhale, exhale while thinking mantra, mantra, mantra, and then inhale again. This might sound a little weird to you but in practice it's very easy and calming. Your mind may well drift away from your mantra and you'll start thinking about something, but that's not a problem. As soon as you become aware of it, or that the mantra has gone, don't be angry or frustrated. Just calmly come back to the mantra and carry on again.

Because of my personality, I always want to analyse and understand things. I think the mantra has to be a meaningless word so that you're unlikely to start thinking about something. If it was someone's name, for instance, or an object you were using as your mantra, you'd likely think about the person or the object, which defeats the purpose. Also, if you don't sit up but lie down instead, you may fall asleep, which might seem like a positive thing but you're not able to control your mind in sleep, so it doesn't get the switch-off time it needs.

If you'd like to try this yourself, I would urge you to research the different types of meditation available, try some free guided meditations and maybe attend a course delivered by an experienced teacher.

Becoming conscious of negative thoughts and thought patterns is a useful skill to develop. Very often I can find myself thinking into the future and worrying about what might happen. This can become draining and lead to increased emotional stress as you agonise over and over again about the "what if?" scenario, when maybe you have little or no influence over it. You've probably worried about similar things numerous times at various stages of your life and they've never come to fruition, but still you worry. Even if they do come true, several weeks or months later, you've forgotten all about them and the negative emotions you had at the time seem like a distant memory.

In times of uncertainty for me, I remember two things. The first is a question: "Why is this happening *for* me?" This is a technique advocated by author and life coach Tony Robbins and helps to provide distance between you and the situation you're in. Rather than asking, "Why is this happening *to* me?" which puts you in the middle of it and forces you to become the helpless victim of the circumstance, it makes you see it from the outside and understand how you're going to benefit as a result of the lessons you'll learn during the experience.

Example

A project you're responsible for has gone horribly over-budget because of unforeseen circumstances.

The old you may have asked, "Why has this happened? Why me?" You become responsible for it and beat yourself up. You focus on any negatives and tell yourself you're not very good.

The new you will ask, "Why has this happened *for* me?" What lessons are you learning as a result of this that will enable you to be better next time? How have you grown during this process?

The second thing I remember is simply: "This too will pass." On many occasions throughout my life I've been under stress or have made mistakes, and I'm still here. The possible calamity I was spending far too many hours thinking about at the time either never materialised or, if it did, I got through it and learnt from it. Whatever the current stressful situation, it will pass and, in a few months' time, it will be a distant memory just like all the other stressful situations that are in your past. I'm not advocating that you become complacent or ignore things that matter, or that you walk around with a permanent, false smile when inside you're going crazy. I'm just suggesting you get better at noticing negative thoughts and worries, try to put them into perspective and decide what meaning you're going to attach to them.

Gratitude

As much as your life may feel stressful sometimes and things can get on top of you, there are always things to be genuinely grateful for. Positive things are happening around you all the time but when you become locked into a loop of focusing on the negatives internally, you miss and ignore them. A good tool you can use is to journal every day. Buy a simple, blank notepad and, at the end of each day, write down the things you did and your thoughts on them. Allow yourself to dump the contents of your mind onto the page and see what happens. Once you've finished, write down at least three things you are grateful for that day. They can be small or profound, but write them down.

You may feel you have nothing to be grateful for as you've had the most horrible, stressful day. But the very fact you woke up this morning is something to be grateful for as many people didn't, or that the sun was shining and the birds were singing because spring is on its way. It might be that a colleague said something positive about you today, or that you're in a great relationship with someone. There are many things, and people, that are very positive in our lives and we often take them for granted. But we'd be better served if instead we were grateful for them.

In our clinic we have a gratitude jar. It's just a glass jar that has some small slips of blank paper clipped to the top. Whenever someone in the team notices something they are grateful for about their work, a patient or another member of the team, they write it down on a slip and put it into the jar. Noticing these positive moments in your life will help remove the influence that negative things have and will release happy hormones. It will encourage you to remain focused on the positive aspects of your life.

However, the real power comes about 12 months later when you allow yourself to read your previous journal entries or pick a few slips from the jar. You'll be reminded of the situations you've overcome, the many positive things in your life and your achievements from the previous period that you'd forgotten about. It can be very empowering and make you realise that, instead of being a victim of circumstance, you are strong and can overcome many obstacles when necessary.

If you feel comfortable sharing your journal entries with family, do so. And if you have a family gratitude jar, at the end of the year empty it out and read the contributions all together. The family bonds you have will be strengthened as everyone realises the potential positive impact simple daily actions have had on each other, and getting recognition for them is very enjoyable too.

Thinking positively and not allowing negative things to take over is undoubtedly an important aspect of health. Some time back, I made a decision to stop reading the national papers or watching the news. It became apparent that it was generally all negative and there was little I could do about it. Having all this negativity pushed into my consciousness wasn't helping me in any way and it was obvious that the majority of news sources have all got their own agendas to push, often with a political or profit-increasing bias. Extreme, sensational headlines sell more papers or garner higher viewing figures and hence make more profits. I believe that consuming large quantities of the output of these sources is a way of controlling the masses so they believe and act in certain ways. Often, only one side of a story is reported and different viewpoints are ignored as they don't fit the bias being pushed.

My advice is, unless tackling an issue is important to you and effecting change becomes your source of empowerment, choose wisely the thoughts and ideas that you allow others to place into your mind.

CHAPTER 5

Unsafe Toxins

We now know that over the past several million years, the species of animal known as human has evolved a set of genes or recipes that have been shaped by the environment they found themselves in at various stages throughout that time. The foods they ate, the liquids they drank, the air they breathed and the way they acted, moved and thought - all these influenced the current human genome such that it had the best possible chance of survival and of passing on its genes to the next generation through procreation, as long as they were exposed to that same environment.

For the best chance of survival, we need to mimic the environment of our ancestors as closely as we can and provide our genes with what they are expecting. It follows, then, that to increase the odds of success, by which I mean health, we should also ensure that any things our genes have never been exposed to, have no need for, or indeed have no mechanism to deal with should be avoided.

Everything you expose your body to can be thought of as either beneficial or harmful. If it's something your body requires for health and your genes have been adapted for over the previous thousands of generations of your family, then it's beneficial. If your genome has no need for it, it brings no advantage to have it in your body and you have to "deal" with it, it's harmful.

If your genes require vitamins, minerals and micronutrients from plants, roots and fruits, then eating them can only drive you closer to health. If your body has no use for pesticides or the chemicals found in cleaning products or drugs, for example, then exposure means it has to attempt to deal with and remove them, and you are moving further away from health. There are obviously varying degrees of benefit or harm depending on the substance, its potency and the exposure, but the beneficial or harmful rule still applies.

Example 1

You eat a meal of organic vegetables in a salad dressed using olive oil and a little lemon juice, with some naturally reared meat and a glass of pure, filtered water. Your body needs the nutrients found in the foods and knows exactly what to do with them. The abundant vitamins, minerals, protein, carbs and fats are shipped off to wherever they are needed to either fuel your body or heal and repair it. The water is used to hydrate your body and your health status is improved. Your genes and those of your ancestors have been relying on and expecting all the components of your meal, and your body knows exactly what to do with them and how to process them.

Example 2

You eat a meal of a pizza that came from a box in the freezer aisle, with some chips and a glass of diet cola. The vegetables and meat on the pizza are from conventional farming practices complete with chemical fertilisers, pesticides and antibiotics. The base of the pizza is made of wheat, stabilisers and improvers. The ingredients on the box read like a chemistry experiment and 75% of them don't sound like "food". The chips are deep fried in a chemically extracted vegetable oil that has been heated beyond safe temperatures to create inflammation and cancer-causing compounds. The diet cola has virtually nothing in it that exists in nature and is a chemical concoction of artificial ingredients.

Your stomach begins to digest the meal and, as all the unnatural elements enter your bloodstream, your body recognises them as toxic and starts to deal with them, filtering them out and attempting to remove as much as possible through your pee, your poop and your skin. Fortunately, it's extremely good at doing this and almost all of it is removed, although some remains; along with the damage that was caused while the toxins were in your blood and brain. The few nutrients that were extracted that are actually required for health are moved around your body to wherever they are needed. You've received energy from the calories in the meal but little by way of nutrition.

Example 3

You run a hot bath and, while it's filling, you pour in some strong-smelling bath foam. The steam rises and the bubbles form, making it very inviting. The scent is unfortunately from a petrochemical source and is toxic so, as you inhale, your lungs pass the toxins into your bloodstream and they find their way quickly all around your body. You slide into the lovely warm water and feel the heat relax your muscles from the strains of the day. But your skin is porous, so it immediately starts to allow the chemicals in the bath foam to find their way into your bloodstream again, along with the chlorine and fluoride in the water. These chemicals circulate around your whole body and it begins to filter them out, although some tiny traces will remain.

Example 4

You have a headache. It's been there on and off for several days and seems to be getting worse. You reach for the paracetamol and swallow two down. Your stomach dissolves the tablets and the drugs enter your bloodstream. The pain signals that alert your brain to a problem are slowly switched off until the pain cannot be felt anymore. Your liver has to filter the drugs from your bloodstream as they are recognised as a toxic invader. The lack of pain signal allows you to carry on doing the thing that originally caused the pain, for example, sitting at a poorly laid-out workstation, and you're not aware of the further damage you are causing. The muscles and ligaments around your neck and head become slightly tighter than they were and the headache returns a few hours later, once the pain signals are no longer numbed by the drugs. You are moving further away from health.

I realise that some of these examples may make me sound like an uptight, miserable killjoy who doesn't know how to enjoy himself, but I make no apologies for them! They are also very simplistic in terms of your body's function, but I've included them purely to illustrate the point that everything you do can be considered as either beneficial or harmful when you analyse what is happening.

All the toxins you are exposed to on a daily basis, from your food and drink, to the household products you use and the medications you take, are probably classed as safe by government guidelines. The manufacturers will have conducted research on the particular ingredient or chemical with the sole intention of proving their product is OK for use so that it can be sold at a profit. However, as mentioned in chapter 2, this will have been done for a limited time and in isolation. No studies are ever done to check the consequences of exposure to multiple toxins at the same time, and for many, many years. How could they be? There would have to be studies of millions of people with different levels of exposure to different groups of toxins, and for tens of years, to determine if the thing in question was still safe long term.

So a balance has to be struck and assumptions made to enable products to get to market in a reasonable time. We know that many of these chemicals are unsafe at certain exposures. Permission to use them is therefore gained as long as they are below a "safe" maximum level. But this only means that you probably won't notice any ill effects short term. Using the product doesn't immediately cause symptoms or kill you. The safe level also can't take into account the impact of multiple similar carcinogenic or hormone-disrupting chemicals being in your system at the same time, or the differing effects that may arise from mixing two or more of these substances together in your body.

Pharmaceutical medications are given to us in increasing amounts and we trust the person who writes the prescription to know that they are safe. There is always a list of possible side effects included in the packet but how often do you read it? When you do read some of them, you may ask yourself, "Why would anyone take this?" They just sound so frightening. But we do and more so than ever. For instance, did you know that reactions to properly prescribed prescription medications are the third leading cause of death in the USA, behind heart disease and cancer! Just think about that: these are not illegal drugs bought on the street or over the internet, these are properly prescribed by a doctor, who took into account all their training, experience and the contraindications of the package insert, but people still die in their thousands. No mistake has been made; no one is to blame. It was just a reaction to the drug.

More people die from these reactions than they do from diabetes, Alzheimer's and stroke, for instance! To make it worse, it's often your body that does the actual healing while the drug just reduces the symptoms so you're not aware while it's happening. Yet we credit the drug with being the thing that fixed you.

You can't put health in a pill and bottle it; the pill didn't make you healthy. Only your body can restore health but, as we now know, the level of success is dependent on the environment we provide it with.

Vaccinations

Vaccinations are a very contentious area of public concern, with a growing number of people questioning their effectiveness and safety. If anyone speaks out against vaccinations, they are deemed to be unscientific and scaremongering. You can probably guess where my thoughts lie on this subject. Your genes do not need vaccinations for health but I can understand why a parent may choose to vaccinate their children.

Julia and I deliberated for a long time about the issue and read a lot of different viewpoints before choosing to avoid all vaccinations for our son. If vaccinations were 100% safe and had no possible ill effects, even though they're not always that effective, I would probably have thought, "Why not?" However, like any prescription medication, vaccinations have side effects and some of them are too tragic to think about. Knowing what I do, I couldn't have lived with myself if I had agreed to having my son vaccinated and he had suffered a life-changing or health-damaging reaction. How could anyone? All the information about possible side effects is within the leaflet in the packaging and you still said, "Yes, take the chance."

It must be heartbreaking for the parents of vaccination-injured children. Vaccination doesn't actually provide lifetime immunity like catching the disease does either, and many kids who have had vaccinations still get measles, chicken pox or mumps but in later life, when the symptoms are worse, giving a greater chance of serious consequences. Vaccination advocates will point to the rates of infection that have dropped significantly since they were introduced, but what they don't point out is that there has only been a tiny drop in cases since vaccinations and that, in reality, clean water and proper sanitation had already had a massive impact on the diseases before they were introduced.

Seasonal flu vaccinations are no better. To be effective, the vaccine manufacturer must predict which type of flu is going to be prevalent that year and then produce the correct vaccination to suit. There are so many variants of flu circulating around the world, and they are mutating all the time, that it is very difficult to get it right. So very often, the people who have had the flu vaccination still get flu but of a different strain to the one they were protected against. However, the vaccinations do make a massive amount of money for the drug companies!

No randomised double blind trials have ever been done on the safety and effectiveness of vaccinations, as it's seen as unethical to give someone a fake placebo vaccination and then compare the results with those of another person given a real one. Also, no one is checking for the effect of multiple doses of an increasing number of vaccinations in a short space of time. All that happens is that rates of vaccination are compared with rates of disease and adverse reactions. But correlation does not mean causation. That is, just because the rates of disease are falling, it doesn't mean it's as a result of the vaccinations.

The decision to vaccinate is definitely a personal one and I don't intend to influence your choice one way or another. I'm not qualified to do so. The majority of people who receive vaccinations don't appear to have any immediate ill effects, so they or their parents are understandably pro-vaccination. But speak to the parents of a vaccination-injured child who died or whose personality changed overnight after vaccination and you get an entirely different opinion because of their experiences. They live with regret, guilt and anger because of a lack of information. It's a classic example of reductionist thinking: measuring and considering only one thing in isolation and not caring about the effect on anything else. The child may not get mumps or measles but, as a result of the ingredients in the vaccination, they could later suffer other things, such as seizures, allergies or numerous auto-immune conditions. However, if all you're measuring is the measles infection rates, then the vaccination is a success!

Reductionism is widespread in healthcare unfortunately, and another example to illustrate this happened at my little boy's nursery. A dentist had come along to talk to the children about the health of their teeth and how they needed to brush them properly (to counteract today's modern diet, but that's a topic for another time), which is a great idea. During the visit, the dentist realised that the children had been given a piece of fruit to eat mid-morning as a healthy snack. Because of his reductionist view - only being concerned with their teeth - during his visit he chastised the nursery staff and told them that the acid in the fruit would damage the children's teeth. He said they should give the kids bread sticks as a snack instead!

So, wait a minute... breadsticks are better than fruit? To the dentist, the logic of this seemed sound. He looks after kids' teeth and fruit acid can erode tooth enamel. But compare the two things side by side, taking a holistic view, and decide which option is best for the overall health of the child. Is it the bread stick comprised of highly processed grains, devoid of any significant nutritional value, with all the added preservatives and other chemicals needed to keep it fresh for months? Or could it be the piece of natural fruit, simply picked from a tree, containing all the vitamins and minerals that humans have evolved to thrive on over the last few million years? Which of these two options moves your child closer to health and which one moves them away? Needless to say, we asked that our son continued to be given the fruit.

I would urge you to read about vaccinations, both for and against them, and use some logical thought to come to a decision that's right for you. Take a holistic view. Don't be bullied by anyone to make a decision one way or another, as there is a lot of that from both sides of the argument, but instead come to your own decision.

It's not just food and drink

Obviously, a significant part of what we put into our bodies on a daily basis is the foods we eat and the liquids we drink, so keeping them as toxin free as possible is a great idea. However, these are not the only things we put into our bodies, as I've already alluded to. You are constantly exposed to a wide variety of potentially harmful substances. I would imagine you clean your house with a range of cleaning products that all do a great job of removing grime, killing bacteria and leaving a pleasant smell behind. But have you ever thought about what's in them and how they could be affecting you? The majority of them are hazardous to the flora and fauna and carry warning labels on the back. You might think that as long as you don't tip them into the nearest river, it'll be fine. Well, it certainly would cause a lot of damage if you did that, or if you accidentally drank a small amount of them. But you also absorb them into your body through your skin or breathe them in in the form of a vapour. If you don't wear gloves you will definitely allow a small amount into your bloodstream, as your skin is permeable.

If that sounds unbelievable, just think about medications that are applied through skin patches, such as morphine and other pain killers, or nicotine patches to help a smoker kick the habit. You're absorbing things through your skin all the time and it has no idea what it should avoid; it all goes in! The same goes for airborne vapours from cleaning products. If you can smell them, they're already in your lungs and being absorbed into your bloodstream. I don't mean to sound alarmist, and the amounts are obviously very small, but it is happening. The longer you have your bare hands in a bucket of cleaning products, or the longer you breathe in the smell of bleach, the greater your exposure.

Your toiletries are the same. Sometimes a long soak in a hot bubble bath after a hard day is just what's needed. As I've already talked about, unconsciously, you pour a chemical cocktail of petroleum products and probable carcinogens into hot water and breathe in the vapour of artificial fragrances that rise in the steam. Then you sink into the warm water and the pores of your skin open up. Immediately, your skin begins to absorb whatever is in the water, regardless. Fortunately, your body has the ability to filter it out and remove it but some residues can remain.

Now I know you may again be thinking this is over the top, but I believe that's probably just your perception as we're so used to doing this sort of thing - and it *feels* nice. But picture a beautiful, crystal-clear, pure mountain stream, running through an untouched landscape. You fill a bath with this water, then heat it gently. You've had a long day and it looks so inviting. It's the perfect temperature and, as the steam rises slowly from the surface, you know you want to get in.

Although you can feel the steam in your nose, it has no actual smell until someone comes along and puts a few drops of chlorine and fluoride in it. Now there is a faint smell, reminiscent of a swimming pool or bleach. Then they open a bottle that has hazard warnings all over the label declaring that it is dangerous for wildlife and a possible carcinogen, and they add a few drops of that too. The aroma changes again and it begins to smell more unpleasant. However, now there are bubbles in your bath. Lastly, another bottle with warnings on it is opened and some of the contents added. And the smell changes to something a little better, possibly lavender or pine.

Now that you've seen the perfect, pure water being tainted by the chemicals, do you still want to get in it and soak for an hour? Would you put your children in it? Or would you prefer the bath before the chemicals were added? The only thing that is different about this compared to the average bath any of us might take for the majority of our lives is that we've actually seen the chemicals being added. Our perception has been altered by this. Normally the chlorine and fluoride are added at the water treatment plant and the bubble bath bottle has pictures of flowers or nature on it. We pour it in and the bubbles appear but we rarely think about what is actually in it.

We spray chemical mists of air fresheners into our homes and even allow little devices to do it automatically for us. We then inhale the vapour and absorb it into our bloodstreams where, hopefully, our bodies will remove it all, leaving no residue behind and not being damaged in the process. All we perceive is the smell, without considering the influence of its chemical ingredients on our bodies.

Tooth decay

Fluoride is a known neuro-toxin, meaning that it kills nerve and brain cells. That's not my opinion, it's a confirmed fact. There are warnings all over toothpaste containers about limiting the amount you swallow, especially for children. If your child does ingest fluoride toothpaste, you are advised to take them to hospital because of the potential for nerve damage.

So why, you may ask, if you live in an area that has a fluoridated water supply, are you allowed to ingest an unmetered amount of this neuro-toxin orally? Yes, it passes over your teeth and we're advised that fluoride helps prevent tooth decay and cavities, but you then swallow it and it's absorbed into your body! How can that be a good idea? Good teeth but fewer brain cells!

Your hunter-gatherer ancestors didn't have fluoride and they had strong teeth for their entire adult life. They may not have been perfectly white but they were strong and functional. We would never have thrived and evolved to become the dominant species on the planet if it was normal to lose our teeth through decay in our thirties, forties or fifties. The fossil record shows that early humans frequently survived into their eighties (as long as they weren't killed by predators or didn't fall out of a tree searching for food) and they had strong teeth at the time. They had to be able to eat and they didn't need fluoridated toothpaste or water. The diet they ate didn't cause decay or cavities. If it had have done, they'd have died of starvation, unless either their diet changed or their teeth evolved to cope with their diet.

I'm not suggesting you forgo dental hygiene at all, by the way. I'm just asking you to apply the same logic I've used throughout this book to explore why we do something a certain way and if there is a better, more logical option. I personally choose to use a fluoride-free toothpaste and I've also had a filter installed in my house and at our clinic to remove the bulk of the chlorine and fluoride from our mains water supply. It's been this way for many years and my dental health is really good. I still brush my teeth twice a day, go for my dental check-ups and I rarely have a problem.

The sun doesn't cause cancer

Skin cancer is big news and big business. For around the past 25 to 30 years, the message we've heard is that you need to cover up, keep out of the sun and make sure you wear a sunblock or high factor sun cream. Often cosmetics have an SPF (sun protection factor) too as this is seen as a good thing and a benefit to choosing one product over another. There are so many tanning lotions available and it's a multi-million-pound industry, all sold to us under the belief that the sun is harmful and that, if we want to get a tan, we must first cover ourselves in these products.

Well, I don't believe it! The rates of skin cancer are rising steadily yet there are more and more products available and "everyone knows" that you have to use them. Do you think the people who develop skin cancer are the ones who forget to apply enough lotion? And because skin cancer rates are rising, are more and more people forgetting to apply their sun cream? If that were the situation, there would have to be fewer products sold each year and more people deciding not to use them, wouldn't there, to coincide with the rising numbers of cancer cases?

We evolved under the sun. The sun is at the centre of our very existence, both physically and metaphorically, and drives everything on our planet.

Nothing could exist without it and, come the day when it inevitably burns out in a few billion years' time, all life on earth will cease to be.

There are many benefits to sun exposure but a major one to humans is the production of vitamin D. Your skin uses cholesterol in your body to make vitamin D when it is exposed to the sun and adequate amounts of vitamin D are essential to a huge number of the processes in your body. In fact, it is actually not a vitamin at all but a hormone, and there are very few ways to get it in our diet, which makes sun exposure all the more important. Your ancestors didn't use sun cream and would have had a lot of exposure to the sun. However, if they were too hot or felt it burning, they would have sought the shade for a time, which would have made sense. They wouldn't have lain out in it all day!

Inadequate vitamin D has been linked to:

- Osteoporosis and Osteopenia
- Many types of cancer
- Heart disease
- High blood pressure
- Obesity
- Diabetes
- Autoimmune diseases
- Gout
- Infertility and PMS
- Parkinson's disease
- Depression and Seasonal Affective Disorder
- Alzheimer's disease
- Chronic fatigue syndrome
- Fibromyalgia
- Chronic pain
- Periodontal disease
- Psoriasis

A while ago I applied this logic to myself and now rarely use sun cream, unless I know I'm going to be unavoidably exposed for a long period of time and there's nothing I can do about it. This is purely to avoid burning. Like many people, I like to have a sun tan and so, if I'm on holiday and want to relax outdoors, I'll lie in the sun for 20 minutes or so unprotected, but then seek the shade of a parasol or similar. I don't burn, my skin is making vitamin D and I get a great tan. I'm also not covered in a cocktail of who-knows-what chemicals that are being absorbed into my body while I lie for hours, roasting and baking my skin.

There is a growing body of evidence that claims that the increasing rates of skin cancer are due to the increased usage of sun creams and the reduction in vitamin D production. It just seems to make sense to me. It's stupid to keep doing the same things over and over and expect a different outcome but that's what we're told to do. Keep using more and more sun cream, with higher and higher SPF, whilst all the time the skin cancer diagnoses increase! Something is just not right.

Chemical foods

Modern food "products" (and I use that word deliberately as I don't consider them to be just "food") are a toxic concoction of chemicals, pesticides, preservatives and artificial substances, all designed to prolong the shelf life, cheapen production costs and ultimately maximise profits. Very rarely is any food manufacturer actually concerned about the nutritional value or benefits to the consumer, unless they can use that information to sell even more. Statements such as "low fat" or "no added sugar" are splashed across the packaging and these are deliberately used to latch on to whatever current food trend the manufacturers think is most likely to make you buy their product. What the packaging doesn't say is "lots of added junk to make it taste OK even though we've removed the fat" or "sweetened using chemical sweeteners that kill brain cells", but that's just as true. That wouldn't make the products sell, though.

I've already talked about the natural diet for the human animal and the foods we ate that shaped our genome, and at no time in our evolution have our bodies been bombarded with such a toxic insult as they are today. We willingly buy these products and eat them under the false impression that they are beneficial to health but it's just a game of smoke and mirrors. Do you ever read the ingredients on the side of food product packaging? It's very rare to find a full list of things you might recognise as food and very often it reads more like a chemistry experiment. Have a look the next time you're in the supermarket aisles. Read the ingredients and, if there's something there that you can't pronounce, doesn't sound like food or would never appear in a recipe book, don't buy it!

When was the last time you saw a TV chef explain that they like to add a teaspoon of "mono and di-glycerides of fatty acids" or read a recipe in a cookery book that calls for "partially inverted sugar syrup, modified maize starch and humectant"? You won't find these for sale in the shops to be used in home cooking so why would we eat them within any other food? One of the worst culprits I've noticed is ready-made sandwiches in the chiller counter of supermarkets. It will take you a few moments to read them but I urge you to have a look. You'll wonder how they manage to fit them all into the little triangular box, there are so many of them!

No human prior to the current generation ate these ingredients and our bodies have not evolved to benefit from them. Give us another 100,000 years or so and, if we're still around, we might have adapted to utilise them but I personally doubt it.

Many people's response to this kind of discussion is that there are toxic chemicals all around us in the form of air pollution, fire retardants and the like, and because you can't avoid them it's pointless to try. I understand this viewpoint. There are so many environmental toxins that we are unknowingly bombarded with daily that it can seem futile to care. In our industrialised societies we are constantly exposed through the air we breathe, the things we eat and drink and the products we put on our skin, and some of it we can have no control over. But there are many things we can control and it's got to be sensible to reduce our exposure by as much as we can, whenever we can.

Choose organic foods whenever they're available on the shelves, even though they cost a little more money. They cost more because it's more expensive to grow them organically and protect them from pests without using pesticides and weed killers. Grow your own if you can. Cook real food from real ingredients and don't buy anything that comes in coloured packaging with a science experiment written on the side. Yes, it can take a little longer and require more thought, but this is your life and your children's lives we're talking about!

Search out your local farmers' market and ask them what they feed their animals. Make sure the animals you eat ate their natural diet and weren't given antibiotics and hormones routinely. I promise you you'll taste the difference in the quality and your health will be better as a result.

Search out a water filter to remove fluoride and chlorine from your drinking water. The majority of filter jugs don't do this but read the list of things they do remove to check. It's more convenient long term to have a whole-house filter installed, so that not only do you cook with and drink filtered water but you also bathe, shower and wash in it too.

If, as a society, we started to choose only real foods, grown and raised naturally, and if we rejected harsh chemical cleaners and toxic toiletries, the more natural alternatives would become more widely available because manufacturers are always watching for emerging trends. If no one ever bought toxic products and they stayed on the shelves, they'd stop making them and switch to making more of the natural things we chose instead. It's already happening slowly as more and more organic and natural choices appear, because more people are rejecting the artificial toxic versions, but let the retailers know that this is what you want by choosing them whenever they're available.

CHAPTER 6

Rest

Adequate rest and recovery time is often one of the most overlooked aspects of a wellness lifestyle. We're slaves to the alarm clock and our days can be manic, filled with work, kids' clubs and keeping on top of things, so we make those days longer and longer by giving ourselves less rest time for sleep and recovery. As the saying goes, we burn the candle at both ends. We haven't got time to sleep!

Well, the reality is we most definitely need sleep; anything from seven to nine hours seems to be the natural norm.

Our time sleeping is organised into blocks of approximately 90 to 120 minutes, termed the sleep cycle. When you first drift off, you're in light sleep but then move to different depths of sleep over the cycle. Towards the end you move from deep sleep to REM sleep, which is a very light, almost awake state of sleep. This is often when we dream and usually the state we're in just before waking. In any night's sleep we'll move through this cycle four to six times and will likely dream in each cycle. However, we'll only normally remember the dreams we had if we woke during them. The dream you remember most vividly is the one you're having as you wake in the morning, or the one you had in the middle of the night that was so unpleasant, it woke you up.

Once someone is in a deep sleep state, it's quite difficult to wake them and, if you do, they'll probably feel a little groggy. If you're someone who always needs an alarm to wake you up for work, the chances are you're not getting enough sleep or you're going to bed too late. And if that alarm wakes you up whilst you're in deep sleep, you'll probably feel grumpy and be accused of "getting out of bed on the wrong side". The easy answer is to go to bed a little earlier but you probably already know that! As a society we're trying to make the night shorter and shorter whilst lengthening the day, because we want to squeeze more "living" into life.

It's unavoidable that you must spend around a third of your life asleep if you want to be happy, well and productive. It's what you've evolved to require over the past few 100,000 years and nothing you do can alter that. Sleep is absolutely essential for health; you can't possibly function properly without it and, in fact, when chronically sleep deprived, you're downright dangerous! Concentration, alertness and all other aspects of mental performance will suffer.

When your early ancestors were in central Africa, their sleep time would have likely been governed by sunrise and sunset, and as there is little seasonal difference when closer to the equator, this amount of time would have been relatively constant. However, as we began to migrate away from the equator, there was an increasing effect from the changing seasons as the winter days became shorter and summer days longer. I realise that my constant thread of logic begins to fall down here as, for instance, in the UK in summer, we only have about six hours of darkness per day, whilst in the winter we have around 15. It would therefore be difficult for our sleep patterns to be governed by dawn and dusk times, although it's potentially what our bodies crave!

My wife has a phrase that has been passed down the generations of her family: "It's the hours before midnight that count." I haven't personally read any science to back this up, and very often sufficient sleep is overlooked in a wellness lifestyle, but I know that in our experience, it's very true. If I have eight hours of quality sleep but didn't go to bed until perhaps midnight, I feel less rested than if I'd had the same eight hours but had fallen asleep at 10pm. With the former, the next day I feel a little sluggish and almost hungover. The effect is cumulative too, so if I have several nights of good sleep in a row, I feel great. However, if I have a number of late nights over a week, I begin to feel lethargic and tired no matter how much sleep I get. There could be good reason for this as your body moves through different phases of rest and regeneration and carries out specific processes throughout your sleep cycle. Reducing the time spent sleeping or having a lot of late nights can have dramatic effects on your wellbeing.

However, what if you already know this and would love to sleep well but struggle to fall asleep or wake up far too early and can't drift off again? There are many potential causes for disrupted sleep, such as stress, anxiety or even your diet.

We all have stresses in our lives but your personal capacity to cope with them is what may lead you to having disturbed sleep. I sometimes find that I can feel physically and mentally exhausted, with heavy eyes that I can barely keep open whilst reading a book. So, I switch off the light and settle down to sleep... and BANG! As soon as my head hits the pillow, my mind begins to race.

I'll start with some silly little mundane thing that needs my attention tomorrow and that leads on to something else, and something else, and before I know it my monkey mind is whirring around seemingly out of control. My heart will start to beat faster and I can hear the pulse in my ears. It's as though someone has flicked a switch in my head and now the heavy eyes have gone and I'm fully alert, almost instantly! In effect, this is what has happened as, during the day, you're distracted from your fears and worries by everything else that you're doing. But at night in bed, there are no other distractions so these thoughts come to the forefront of your mind. In the past, I used to get frustrated and angry that this had happened and would begin tossing and turning, which of course only made things worse and was likely to disturb my wife. Over the years though, I've used a few different approaches to help and I now have a personal strategy to alleviate the effects.

About 30 to 60 minutes before bedtime, I begin to wind down, turning down the lights and ideally turning off the TV or computer. The last room we normally visit before getting into bed is then the bathroom, which is often very brightly lit! So, if you can, create a way of having low light levels in there whilst brushing your teeth and using the toilet. Bright lights make us more alert and will likely delay sleep.

Once in bed, my first tip is to have a notebook and pen by my side. I'll jot down whatever the thing is that my mind is fixated on, usually a task that needs doing tomorrow. There might be more than one, or numerous things to write down but I find putting them on paper can help to get them out of my head. If this doesn't have the desired effect, I lie on my back with my arms by my sides and focus on my breathing. Taking slow breaths and concentrating on the feeling of my chest rising and falling, I imagine the bed becoming softer and softer as I exhale and my body sinking into it. Each time I exhale, I get heavier and sink further down into the softest mattress imaginable.

Thinking about nothing is virtually impossible, so I'll think about a piece of blank, white paper that's very close to my face so it's all I can see. It's my personal version of nothing! This is often the last thing I remember doing when I wake the next morning so it obviously works for me. It's actually a kind of mindfulness similar to what I described in chapter 4, because when you allow your mind to race, you'll either be thinking about something that has happened previously that you can't change or something that hasn't happened yet, both of which are pointless. By focusing on your breathing, counting imaginary sheep or sinking into the mattress, you're in the present and very often you'll drift off in a matter of moments.

Another technique that works for many people is to actually do the opposite of what you want to happen. It sounds counter-intuitive but if you're struggling to settle down and fall asleep, lie back and try to stay awake! Keep your eyes open in your darkened bedroom, blink as normal and think about staying awake. When you're already tired, it's exhausting to try to stay awake and you'll often find yourself drifting off to sleep in the process. You're effectively making your mind focus on something other than your worries and stresses, which is often the key.

I'll admit this doesn't work 100% of the time. If I find I still can't relax, rather than get frustrated as I used to, I'll accept it, get out of bed and go downstairs to read, watch TV or write a book! Nothing too stimulating or exciting and I try to keep the light levels low, so perhaps use a low wattage table lamp etc. Personally, I find a warm, caffeine-free drink helps. I eventually feel my eyes becoming heavy again after about 30 minutes and I go back up to bed and drift off. It's obviously not ideal as my total sleep time will be reduced but accepting it and not getting angry leads to better, although shorter duration, quality sleep.

Another cause for struggling to fall asleep can be eating a large meal too close to bedtime. I would try to leave a couple of hours at least between your evening meal and settling down for the night. And I don't suppose I need to tell you about caffeine but try to avoid that after 4pm at the latest. Choose a decaf coffee that's either organic or that specifically uses the Swiss water decaffeination process, as neither of those use harmful solvents in their processes. There are also some foods you can eat that have been shown to help you improve your sleep, such as kiwi fruit or walnuts.

If you have no problem falling asleep but find you wake between 1am and 3am, it's often because your blood sugar has dropped rapidly and so your adrenal glands release cortisol, which wakes you up. Eating the "standard western diet" of grain-based foods with added sugars will give you a spike of high blood sugar, followed by a rapid fall afterwards. If your evening meal is very high in these kinds of carbohydrates or if you snack on sweet foods before bed, you'll experience this rollercoaster effect of blood sugar. And if the crash is deep enough to cause a sufficiently low level of blood sugar, your body may wake you up to rectify it. As a short-term fix, you could have a protein-rich snack at the side of the bed, such as nuts, in case you wake up, which should help restore a more normal blood sugar level and aid you getting back to sleep. However, the best long-term strategy is to improve your diet to remove the high and low blood sugar levels, and also to avoid sugary foods in the last few hours before bed.

I sometimes go for a few days waking up an hour before the alarm and I used to get annoyed about this too. I now use it as an extra hour I wouldn't have had and, rather than getting frustrated, I'll spend the time meditating, exercising or reading. If this happens to you, it's a much more beneficial use of the time than lying in bed asking yourself, "Why have I woken up so early again?" Accept it and use the time well as a gift.

The 5 Rs

So why do we sleep? What actually happens during sleep that wouldn't happen if we just stayed awake constantly?

Reorganisation

Your brain has a chance to consolidate the activities from your day. It organises and processes information, sometimes in the form of dreams.

Regeneration

It's a chance for your body to replace aging and dying cells. Every cell in your body is replaced regularly and a lot of this work happens while you sleep.

Recovery

Depending on how active your day has been, the fuel stores in your muscles will need replenishing and refilling ready for another day of activity when you wake.

Repair

The healing of injured and damaged tissues and the removal of toxins.

Re-inflation

When you lie down, you remove the effect of gravity on your spine and other joints. While you're upright through the day, fluid in your joints is slowly squeezed out because of the load you place on them and this is replaced while you sleep. You're actually slightly taller after a restful night asleep!

Think of sleep as your body carrying out essential maintenance processes that can't be done while you're awake.

One last piece of advice would be to try not to take a nap during the day, if at all possible. And if you simply can't function without a nap because you are very sleep deprived, try to limit it to no more than 20 minutes to avoid going into deep sleep, and keep it in the morning where possible. A nap any longer than this, or later in the day, will likely have a detrimental effect on your ability to sleep properly that night and lead to a downward spiral of poorer sleep.

CHAPTER 7

Activity

The physical exercise you include in your life and the energy you expend going about your day all constitute your activity level. So often, improving one's health is simplified into two areas: eat less and exercise more. Many people see both of these as unpleasant, thinking they mean eating tasteless, boring meals that don't leave you feeling satisfied, accompanied by hours of monotonous sweating and straining in the gym. Exercise is often seen as something we can add into our lives to bring health and mitigate all the other bad stuff we still do: "I'll have some more cake but go for a run tomorrow."

Because eating less and exercising more often lead to weight loss and they're supposed to be good for you, you probably assume that if someone has lost weight or they're already thin, they're healthy. Unfortunately, that's just not true. Being thin doesn't automatically mean being healthy. There are plenty of unhealthy ways to lose weight and be thin. Extreme diets involving meal replacement "products", tablets that stop you absorbing fat and even illegal drugs will all make you lose weight but at the same time lose health too.

These kinds of ways to lose weight are often frowned upon by people, but another unhealthy method that seems to be ignored is chronic over-exercising. I know that may sound counterintuitive, as we hear all the time that exercise is essential for health - and let me assure you that it absolutely, most definitely is - but just because something is good for you, it doesn't mean more is better.

You can't possibly be truly well unless you use your body to carry out the kinds of activities it has evolved to expect but, at the same time, running for hours every week will take its toll on your health eventually. You'll probably end your days with a thin, toned body but perhaps you would have had a few more years with your family if you'd spent fewer years running!

A long time ago when I still had a gym membership, there was a man who seemed to be there whenever I went. Because of my schedule, I was sometimes able to go in the morning and sometimes in the afternoon or evening. It was quite random and I rarely went at the same times each week. However, when I did go, he was just about always there. I only ever saw him on the treadmill. He ran and ran and ran. He was quite tall and extremely lean, with bones seemingly sticking out everywhere and big veins visible on his arms and legs. He was obviously very fit and had trained himself to have incredible stamina, being able to run for hours at a time. However, one day when I went to the gym, there was a memorial poster up on the wall with his photo on it and a moving message saying that he had unfortunately died of a heart attack.

There were a few people standing around the water cooler talking about him. I overhead things like, "He was so fit", "He was so healthy" and, "I used to see him running past my house regularly" (yes, he even ran when he wasn't at the gym!). The general conversation was that it was a mystery why he'd died when he was clearly so fit and "healthy". It made no sense to this group of people and they were questioning whether lifestyle made any difference to health.

Unfortunately for this man, he had possibly fallen under the misconception that being "fit" equated to being healthy and that being "more fit" meant having greater health. The two words always go together, don't they? Fit and healthy. Have you ever heard the phrase "fit and unhealthy"? Probably not, but it applies to many people. Although this man's body was clearly fit as he could run for hours at a time, it sadly wasn't healthy. It was probably starved of nutrients if he was following the outdated advice to consume low-fat foods and "healthy" whole grains, and was likely crying out for more fats, proteins, plants, roots and fruits just to try to repair the damage being caused by his chronic activity levels. Perhaps he had a lot of emotional stress in his life and was a worrier, using the exercise to try to manage that. Or maybe his exercise habits had led to the poor posture and forward head carriage that he had, the latter, as already mentioned, having been shown to be closely linked to an increased likelihood of dying from any cause.

If you're thin, or someone you know is thin, I need you to not just assume that means you (or they) are healthy. If you're able to run a marathon or lift ever heavier weights for hours and hours, it doesn't automatically mean you're healthy. You can be thin and strong but heading for a shortened lifespan. Many thin or athletic people die early of a preventable lifestyle-related disease and those around them can't understand how it happened. When viewed through the lens of mainstream health advice that thin is good, that exercise is good, that a low cholesterol result is ideal, that low-fat dairy and whole grains are healthy, it obviously makes no sense that people die young and only reinforces the myth that cancer, heart disease, diabetes, Alzheimer's and the like are all just genetic, random diseases that you can't do anything to prevent. "Why bother?" people think to themselves. "There's no point as it makes no difference." In fact, usually what's happened is that the person has been eating foods other than those they have evolved to require, whilst potentially over-exercising and not feeding their cells appropriately for that level of activity. Eventually it's caught up with them.

Beyond the moderate amount of activity you need for health, any more just means you become more able to do that particular exercise for longer. It doesn't mean you become healthier and more likely to lead a longer life free from disease. Walking for 30 minutes per day at a brisk pace can have a massive, positive impact on your health outcomes. You don't even need to do it every day! Perhaps just five days per week. However, spending more time every day walking, or walking for several hours once per week, won't bring much greater benefit to your longevity, but it will make you better able to walk long distances. If you enjoy doing that and that's how you want to spend your time, then do it. But don't think it will make you healthier.

The same goes for those people who spend hours every week sweating in the gym, or running for miles and miles. I knew someone who said she liked to be pushed by her personal trainer so hard that she was physically sick. Only at that point did she think she'd trained hard enough!

Beyond the improvements brought about by the amount of exercise your body requires for health, the extra time spent just means you get better able to spend more time doing the activity you're doing. You're kind of stuck in a loop: getting better at doing the exercise so you can keep getting better at doing the exercise - not healthier.

So what's the point, unless you really enjoy it and wouldn't prefer to spend some of that time doing other things with your friends and family, for instance?

Spark

Think of exercise as a nutrient for your brain. When you move the joints of your body through their various ranges of motion, special sensors called proprioceptors send very positive signals back up to your brain via your nervous system. In his ground-breaking book *Spark!* (Quercus, 2010), author John Ratey MD describes many studies that have been done using MRIs of the brains of people who exercise regularly, and their relative performance in academic and cognitive areas of life and health. The results are truly remarkable and I urge you to read his book, as it shows beyond doubt that moderate exercise directly leads to new brain cells being created, new connections between those brain cells forming and a huge reduction in the likelihood of diseases such as Alzheimer's, senility and depression. It reduces the production of stress hormones, such as cortisol, and increases the levels of happy hormones, such as serotonin, to bring huge positive shifts in your mood.

Obviously appropriate activity levels have lots of other benefits and I would imagine that improved brain function wouldn't have appeared in your top five prior to reading this book. I'm sure you're aware of the heart health improvements that come from doing activities that increase your heart rate and make it work a little harder, and you'd probably guess that improved lung function and capacity would be a welcome side effect of the right exercise levels, but there are still more advantages. The health of your joints can improve because you're using them more. Moving your joints through their full range of motion not only sends the positive signals up to your brain but it also stimulates the production of the fluid that lubricates the joints. It's called synovial fluid and is present between the joint surfaces of every joint in your body. It's what keeps the joint surfaces further apart and well lubricated. Coupled with joint health, your flexibility and posture will also improve. You'll feel as if you can stand taller, move more easily and your day-to-day activities won't seem so taxing.

The most profound of the benefits of activity, though, has to be the reduction in insulin resistance. I've mentioned insulin in previous chapters and how one of its functions in the body is to enable the transfer of blood sugar from your circulation to the stores of your body: either into your muscles and stored as glycogen for immediate use to fuel them, or into your body fat to be used at a later date when you need to burn more fuel than you have recently consumed. Insulin resistance, you may remember, is the term used to describe the amount of insulin your tissues need to "see" before taking notice and accepting the excess blood sugar into storage. If you are very insulin resistant, your cells won't "hear" the insulin shouting at them to let the sugar in, so your body will release more and more insulin until they do hear it. Also, a high level of circulating insulin doesn't promote the use of stored body fat as energy in your tissues. This means that you tend to retain the extra fat rather than burning it off, but still feel physically tired once you've used up your muscle's energy stores.

If you have very low insulin resistance, your cells only need a small amount of insulin to be present for them to react and let the sugar in. However, if your blood sugar is constantly kept high because of your dietary choices, leading to your body having to produce more and more insulin, your insulin resistance will increase. In a vicious cycle, more and more insulin will need to be released by your pancreas to cope with the chronically high blood sugar levels, which, in turn, will lead to increased insulin resistance, meaning that even more insulin will be required as time goes on. Eventually, your pancreas won't be able to cope with the need for ever more insulin and your blood sugar levels will become dangerously elevated and out of control. Once this happens and you are no longer able to regulate blood sugar, you are labelled as having Type 2 diabetes.

Another term used to describe insulin resistance is insulin sensitivity: if you have high insulin resistance you have low sensitivity to insulin and vice-versa. Chronically elevated levels of insulin are not only linked to diabetes, though; high-circulating insulin is linked to a vast array of illnesses including high blood pressure, polycystic ovary syndrome, coronary artery disease, cardiovascular disease and many more.

Your sensitivity to insulin is an excellent marker for health and you should aim to be as sensitive as possible. In other words, have very low insulin resistance, as this means that your body only has to release a small amount of the hormone for it to do its job of controlling the level of blood sugar. And because your circulating insulin levels are low, your risk for the other diseases related to them is also decreased.

As mentioned, activity and exercise help to reduce your insulin resistance dramatically, increasing your insulin sensitivity and keeping the amount of circulating insulin in your body low. Therefore, subjecting your body to appropriate levels of activity can help reduce your risk for a number of nasty diseases that are currently leading to the early deaths of the majority of those in the civilised world.

Unfortunately, knowledge such as this can lead you to think that you can ignore the other aspects of a healthy lifestyle and just exercise instead - as if exercise is something you can use to "treat" disease; something you can put into your body to fix it, when in reality a loss of health can be the result of the exercise not being there in the first place. Don't think, "Exercise makes me healthy"; instead think, "Exercise is required for health, so I will obviously be unwell without it." If you can't see a difference between those two statements, please re-read them as they form the foundation of so many aspects of health and a healthy lifestyle.

Health is not a commodity that you can put more of into your body. You don't "put health in". Your body is constantly striving to express perfect health but you need to ensure you give it the ingredients it requires and avoid giving it the things it doesn't.

So, in terms of exercise, make sure you give it appropriate activity as that's what your genome has evolved to expect and require, and avoid a sedentary lifestyle; it has never been exposed to that during the hundreds of thousands of years we've been evolving for. Think of other animals that live in the wild all around you. They expend energy almost constantly, searching for food, building shelter, avoiding predators and raising their young. They never need to go to a gym! Their genes have evolved against that backdrop of activity and it's now what they expect to see. Any other level of activity isn't natural for them and will inevitably lead to less-than-perfect health. This is one of the reasons why, very often, animals taken from the wild and kept in captivity won't be as healthy as they would have been in their natural environment.

We are just another animal species and, of course, we have a genetic requirement for a certain level of activity. Not presenting our genes with this can only lead to reduced function and health. Your ancestors walked everywhere, occasionally ran, climbed and carried heavy loads. Hunting animals, climbing trees for fruits, nuts and eggs, digging plants from the ground, fetching water, carrying children and building shelters all take a lot of effort. You have the same requirements as they did but in your modern, comfortable life, the chances are you have a much more sedentary lifestyle than they did, expending far less energy and probably taking in more calories.

Your ancestors will potentially have had periods of strenuous activity on most days, lifting heavy loads such as firewood, building materials or just their children, then carrying them around. The movement would have sent the positive signals up to their brains to keep them in perfect condition. It kept their joints flexible and lubricated, their hearts well exercised and strong and, by loading their skeletons through lifting heavy things, they signalled their bodies to lay down calcium in their bones to keep them strong too. All the time they were using up any blood sugar for energy, keeping their insulin sensitivity high and their risk of disease low. They were quickly able to burn stored body fat for energy too, once blood sugar and muscle stores were depleted, so they were lean.

This was also the case into later life. The older members of their communities were still active and contributed; perhaps not as much as the younger ones but old age was still a far cry from what we assume it to be nowadays. Can you imagine the average modern 80-year-old walking miles and lifting and carrying firewood, for instance? Probably not.

But all this doesn't have to mean gym membership or running for miles and miles on a treadmill, unless of course that's what you really enjoy. You can incorporate appropriate activities into your daily life with a little bit of thought and planning. A 30-minute brisk walk five times per week has been shown to have an incredible reduction on the risk of developing cancer, heart disease, diabetes and the like, so how about parking the car a couple of miles away from the office and walking in? Or allowing for this extra time on the school run and not jostling to park right outside the school gates but parking a mile away and walking in? Your walking pace should be quite fast, though. There's no need to get out of breath but you do need to get your heart rate up and walk as if you mean it! It's also a great opportunity to spend quality time with your child as you walk together, both getting exercise at the same time. I'll always remember walking to school with my mum. It was just the norm to me, chatting as we walked.

You could commit to spending at least 30 minutes with a friend or neighbour, walking and socialising at the same time. And if you're a dog owner, you have a perfect opportunity to walk for 30 minutes. The bizarre thing is you'll *know* your dog won't be well unless it gets the exercise it needs but you'll forget that the same applies to you. It's not that adding walking into your dog's life makes it healthy, it's that not walking will result in it becoming unhealthy. It's a subtle difference but I promise that it's just the same for you.

There are other simple things you can do to add more activity into your life without having to go to the gym. When faced with the choice between the stairs, the escalator or the lift, take the stairs. Climbing a flight of stairs is a great form of exercise and if you can do it at a pace, all the better. It's often faster than waiting for the lift anyway! It always surprises me at an airport when, having been sitting down for several hours in cramped conditions and just got off the plane, everyone queues up to get on the escalator to take them to passport control. The stairs are often empty and choosing them instead would help to get the blood pumping and your body moving again, not to mention getting you nearer to the front of the queue at the security desk. Your body would be begging you for this opportunity to move.

Similar to the school run example, instead of driving around the supermarket car park looking for the space closest to the entrance, find the spot that's furthest away and drive straight to it. You've probably saved some time finding the space and added the opportunity for a little more fast walking as you cross the car park on foot. Then, when you've finished your shopping and have a heavy trolley to push, you'll walk back to your car, again at speed, but this time you have the added bonus of a little bit of resistance training thrown in for good measure.

I haven't got time for exercise so stop hassling me!

There have been many reports recently about the benefits of short, intense bouts of exercise. This is usually called something like high-intensity interval training (HIIT) and comprises doing several short bursts of an activity, such as running or cycling, at your absolute maximum capacity for about 30 seconds or so, interspersed by perhaps 60 or 90 seconds of rest. This is repeated a few times, perhaps up to eight, in quick succession. There are great benefits to this format of exercise in terms of health with the huge bonus that it takes a lot less time to do it and, depending on which activity you choose, you'll need very little, if any, equipment.

If you have a smart phone, there are many free apps you can use that will guide you through this kind of exercise routine. The one I've used the most is called "Max Capacity Training". It only takes 16 minutes to do three times per week and it comprises a variety of bodyweight exercises that you can do at home. There are many others to try, though, so have a look for one that feels right for you and get ready to feel stronger and healthier.

I can see how this form of activity, intense and in short bursts, might be what we've been genetically selected to require. Your ancestors could quite easily have required a similar pattern of energy expenditure at various times through their days. Maybe they had to climb up a succession of trees to reach nuts or fruits, walking between each one, or perhaps they had to fetch firewood in batches, making several trips to and from the source. Hunting animals could have consisted of periods of walking and stalking before sprinting for short bursts to catch them and so on. All this would have required body-weight type exercise.

None of these ideas are designed to give you a "perfect" body, they're just to help you incorporate more activity into your busy life. The media fools us into believing that having a six pack and low body fat are what's important and that that means being healthy, but it's really not true. There are so many unhealthy ways to lose body fat and increase muscle definition and none of them will reduce your risk for disease or increase the length of your productive life. In fact, many of them will actively reduce your health and life expectancy. As you now know, how someone's body looks doesn't always convey the truth about their health. Yes, exercise is extremely important for health but not because it can help make you leaner. You can't out-exercise a bad diet. If you put the wrong foods in leading to the cells of your body being literally starved of nutrients, you can exercise as much as you like and it won't make you healthier. Thinner maybe but not healthier. How could running for longer ever replace the vitamins and minerals in a big, colourful plate of salad and naturally reared meat?

Lastly, wearing a simple activity tracker or pedometer can help you see just how active or inactive you've been on any particular day. They're relatively inexpensive and, although not essential, can motivate you to increase your exercise day by day. Depending on your current activity, set yourself a reasonable starting target of perhaps 6,000 to 8,000 steps per day and work up to 10,000 or more. If you notice that your total is low at any point, aim to schedule in a quick walk to boost it back up and reach your daily target. Give appropriate activity the priority it deserves.

CHAPTER 8

Love and Connection

This might seem to some people as not important, or unrelated to health. To others it could appear to be a bit wishy-washy or "new-age". Go back a few years and I would definitely have been in this camp. Back then I assumed and believed, like many others, that the human body was just a biomechanical machine, and that although love and a connection with others might feel nice, they wouldn't have any physical effect on my health. However, I've very much changed my opinion on this and have already touched on it in chapter 4, "Thoughts".

Your ancestors worked co-operatively in a tribe of perhaps 100 people or more and they were all connected by the common goals and needs of the community. There would have been several family units within the tribe but they would all have worked together to ensure the best chance of survival for everyone. The men would have hunted in packs and co-operated closely to ensure a better chance of success and therefore survival for the tribe. Existing skills and any new innovations would have been passed between them, so the chance of a successful hunting trip would have increased.

A lone hunter would have had a lower chance of success and be limited to the type and size of animal he could hunt. His family would have had access to meat less often. He would only have been as good as the skills he personally possessed, whereas a group would raise the skill levels of all the members and also be able to hunt and carry home larger prey, meaning animal protein would be available more often.

The women would have worked co-operatively with foraging and gathering plants and fruits in groups. They would have been able to do this whilst pregnant, nursing babies or with small children; probably all three at once! Now, I realise this could be a tricky area from a sexism point of view and the role of the genders, but the evidence is clear that the women cared for the children together whilst carrying out the tasks they could do at the same time. These are clearly essential functions they had evolved to do and, again, the best chance of survival was gained by working together, caring for all the children as a group and collecting foods for everyone. The more experienced women of the group would have been able to pass on their wisdom and knowledge, offering support and guidance, nursing others' babies if possible, all the while increasing the chance of survival and thriving for the group as a whole.

The quality of these people's shelters and their physical security would have been improved by everyone working together and sharing knowledge and new innovations. Protection from predators could be offered by working together to ensure the safety of the entire group.

There would have been leaders in the tribe and these were probably made up of the elders of the community, as they carried wisdom, knowledge and experience. Both male and female elders would have been valued and respected because they were the only way that skills could be passed down through the generations – there were obviously no books or formal means of recording them. Valuing and respecting the most experienced members of the community would lead to a tribe having the greatest chance of success and survival, resulting in an increased likelihood that they would produce children.

The main focus for any organism is to survive long enough to be able to reproduce and ensure the continuation of their species by passing on their genes to the next generation. As I've mentioned frequently in this book, those genes were shaped over many previous generations and were expecting the environment to which they were going to be subjected to be within certain parameters. If those parameters were different to the norms and the animal was not able to adapt to the new environment, that particular species would have had a lower chance of survival and therefore be less likely to reproduce. Their particular set of genes, as individual and unique as their fingerprints, would die with them and not live on in their offspring. So, any early humans who chose to live in isolation, or were perhaps cast out of their tribe for some reason, would have had a lower chance of survival, not only because of the physical advantages of working together but also because their genes weren't suited to living alone.

Working in co-operation with others, contributing to a society while feeling safe and loved, all result in certain hormones being released into your body. These are happy hormones, of success and security. Not having these hormones but instead having those of fear, anxiety and isolation can only be tolerated by your body for a limited period of time before health challenges appear. As with most areas of health I've discussed so far, you probably wouldn't immediately begin to see changes in your wellbeing as your body can adapt to a wide range of environmental challenges. However, these adaptations are only sustainable for a limited time and are in place to allow you enough opportunity to change your environment from one of sickness and surviving to one of wellness and thriving.

You may be in the fortunate position of having a large, close family unit around you that offers guidance and support, along with some close friends whom you have a similar relationship with. Perhaps you volunteer your time at a community project or organisation that works together for the common good. If you can see similarities between your current social and family life and the lives of your distant ancestors in terms of support, closeness and contribution, then this aspect of your environment is probably working for you. If, however, you realise that you're living in isolation, either physically or just through a lack of connection to those around you, and you don't feel as if you contribute to anyone or anything, your health could probably benefit from making some changes.

You could find out if there are any organisations around you that need volunteers. Offer your time to a charity or community project and you'll find you have skills or experience that could be of benefit to someone in need. Your local council will be able to help you find some local causes. You'll bring much needed help to others whilst at the same time getting the health benefits yourself.

You could lead a community project such as litter-picking in the streets or perhaps planting flower troughs where you live for the enjoyment of others. Getting others to help will not only build a community but could also be a source of exercise for them!

Ask yourself, "What could I do for you?" expecting nothing in return. You'll make someone else's life better while improving your own feelings of self-worth. Prepare a meal for a neighbour for no other reason than to see the look of gratitude on their face, or share some fruit from your garden. Offer to help an elderly neighbour with their shopping. Or perhaps you could organise a street party and ask each household to bring one dish that can be shared by everyone else. Great memories and bonds are made at events like this. It can really increase everyone's feelings of belonging and being part of a community.

Be Kind

We hold regular team coaching and training days within our clinic and have enjoyed many activities in the past. However, the one that really stands out because we all had such a great time doing it was based on "random acts of kindness". The team was divided into four groups, with each group given five tasks to complete:

1. Let someone go before you in a queue
2. Buy a stranger a coffee
3. Give a bunch of flowers to someone you don't know
4. Place a lottery ticket under the windscreen wiper of a car chosen at random
5. Pick up litter for 15 minutes.

After the task was completed, everyone was buzzing about how it had made them feel and how they wanted to do it again. Can you imagine the extra happy hormones that were flooding through their bodies, not to mention the reduction in stress levels!

Some people can live in fear of their neighbours and in isolation. How many of your close neighbours do you know by name and have a connection with, even if it's just a friendly chat over the fence? Perhaps in this era of social media and reality TV you know more about some vacuous celebrity than you do about the person who's lived over the road from you for years. There is often a great outpouring of grief when someone in the media you've never met and who had no idea you even existed dies. Flowers are sent, cards are written and news reports follow. Yet perhaps you don't know the first thing about the person who lives a few doors down from you and whom you see every day on your way to work.

Social media can seem like a real connection with others but, in many cases, it's just not serving you. It can suck in hours of your life and, as with other types of media, it has generally been turned into a vehicle for someone to push their opinion or agenda onto you with the aim of making money from you or influencing your decisions.

I'm aware that this is a short chapter but that by no means reflects the relative importance or influence over your health that a feeling of connection can bring to you and those around you. Your health is impacted not only by the missing happy hormones that your genome is expecting and the sense of purpose that a real connection provides but also by the chronic increase in stress hormones that isolation and fear create. Connecting with others and collaborating for the benefit of the common good sounds like a selfless thing to do but, in reality, you get massive personal gains so it's truly a win-win!

To learn more about the positive effects of creating and maintaining human connections, I would recommend you read the book *Lost Connections* by Johann Hari (Bloomsbury Publishing, 2019).

CHAPTER 9

The Close

This book will have given you a brief introduction to the main areas of lifestyle that I'm certain are responsible for the majority of health or sickness you will experience in your life. We've discussed Nutrition, Alignment and Posture, Thoughts, Unsafe Toxins, Rest, Activity and finally Love and Connection. My intention has not been to give a prescription of health advice like so many other self-help and health books I've read. Suggestions such as "eat this food to be healthy" or "do this exercise to be healthier" are all well and good but they reinforce the myth that we are flawed in some way and that adding healthy things makes us healthier.

This is, of course, true on the whole but, by framing it in this manner, readers are misled about why they may find themselves with a lack of health in the first place. People don't become sick through bad luck, bad genes or random chance. People become sick because they repeatedly deprive their bodies of the essential ingredients they require to thrive, whilst at the same time bombarding themselves with a huge array of things that their bodies then have to deal with. Sickness is not a physical thing that comes along and attaches itself to you. Sickness is a state of physiology that's developed because your body has begun to break down in the face of an overwhelming lack of what it needs to express health.

If you topped up the fuel tank of your petrol car but accidentally put diesel in instead of petrol, the engine may start but it wouldn't run properly. It would probably misfire and not accelerate like it normally does. You'd have to get the fuel tank drained and refilled with petrol for it to work properly again. Does the petrol give more power to the car or can it not run correctly without the correct fuel? You wouldn't think that the car was flawed and the petrol cured it. You'd know that it had broken down as a result of the incorrect, illogical ingredient you'd added that it wasn't designed to handle. The myriad functions of your body are exactly the same and this book contains what I am certain are the correct ingredients, governed by millions of years of evolution, to allow your body to express health.

By addressing these areas of our lives, the choices you and I make as individuals every day have the potential to positively impact not only our health and that of our families but also the planet, for generations to come. We're sold artificial foods, drinks and other products with slick and manipulative advertising campaigns and we consume them without thinking about the impact. Your body digests them or absorbs them and then processes them. Your level of health is slightly reduced but usually not by an amount you are conscious of.

Ultimately, these artificial products end up in the water, air and soil. Then they infiltrate every living thing on the planet. Any beneficial things that are required for health are used by your body and may become part of you, for instance some protein or calcium. The calories are utilised as fuel and the waste products excreted. Hopefully, the toxic things are filtered out by your body and excreted too. But whatever you flush down the toilet, pour down the drain or retain in your body will eventually find its way into all the other organisms that we share Earth with.

Until a few hundred years ago, everything was naturally occurring, organic, free range or wild. There was no other choice. You could drink the water from a stream safely without the fear of chemicals from the farmland having leached into it; without drug residues and hormones being present and goodness knows what other toxic substances. You could dig foods from the ground and eat them in safety.

Now, artificial foods laced with petro-chemical fertilisers and poisonous pesticides are accepted as the norm and are even described as "conventionally grown" – whereas organic and free-range products, just by the very labelling, are seen as unusual and unconventional, and those who choose these options a little bit weird. They're told they're wasting their effort and money by searching out organic options. They're being ripped off; it's all a scam; they're suckers!

Just as your body is a perfectly organised eco-system of cells working in harmony, so is the planet. Earth is the largest recycling depot imaginable, constantly striving for balance and harmony. The individual atoms that have made up every plant and animal that has ever existed are all still here and are either in the ground, in the air, in the seas or are part of another plant or animal. Similarly, every drug, every bit of plastic or man-made product is still hanging around and waiting to decompose back to its constituent parts over the next few thousand years.

All the atoms that make up your body have previously been part of countless other organisms since time began. As James Chestnut told me, "We are all just animated earth". When you eat a plant or another animal, your body breaks it down and either uses it or filters it out. It's just a matter of time before it winds up back in the soil, water or air to be taken up by the next user that ingests it. Whatever you poop or pee out eventually goes back to the soil and water and when you die, the atoms that made up your body will find their way there too as the body decomposes... all ready for the next generation of flora and fauna to ingest, absorb and utilise, before then returning to where they came from again. Every element and mineral that once made you is recycled and made available for use by something else. And so it goes on and has done forever, and will continue to do so forevermore.

The calcium in your spinach or cabbage was once eaten by a Neanderthal as part of another food. Then it went back to the soil through some form of decomposition, ready to be taken up by the next plant that grew. A mammoth came along and ate the plant, utilising the calcium to grow its bones perhaps. Eventually it then died and decomposed to dust, to be reabsorbed.

The water on the planet, in the oceans and rivers, in the ice caps and clouds, has always been here. It is a closed loop system; a finite amount. Every day you drink water that was once dinosaur tears or rain that fell during the very first storm that ever raged as part of our planet's formation. It's all been used by every plant, animal or microscopic bacteria that have ever lived. It follows then that if we produce toxic wastes as part of some industrial process, or ingest large amounts of artificial foods and pharmaceuticals, they are going to find their way into the planet's ecosystem and therefore into every organism that makes up that system. That includes you, me and all our children.

There have already been many mass extinctions in our planet's history. Thousands of species of highly successful animals that were evolving and thriving together have all been and gone. They'd been around for many more millions of years than we've existed but then disappeared virtually overnight, and the same thing will one day happen to us. We think we're clever and extremely important and just assume that we'll always be around, but in reality life is fragile. We think nature doesn't apply to us and that we've mastered it so we can live our lives however we want, then cure our problems with a gadget or a drug or a chemical. We think we've evolved beyond nature because we're so clever, which is actually very stupid. The dinosaurs were around for about 165 million years, which is over 800 times longer than we have been, but now they're all dust, decomposed and recycled, absorbed by the plants and animals that came next.

Humanity could so easily go the same way and, in a few more million years, virtually no trace of us might exist but the planet would still remain. The ecosystem of Earth would survive, allowing the next wave of life to emerge and evolve to thrive in the environment that exists at that time. The atoms that made up the dinosaurs, that then made up you and me, would become part of another as yet unevolved organism, and so the recycling continues.

I realise I'm painting a bleak picture and I apologise for that. However, this is the reality of how we're living at this moment: above nature, full of self-importance and not bound by its rules. Happy to keep consuming with no thought for the consequences and not living our lives consciously. I'm not saying that we have to live in a cave and forgo all modern comforts. I appreciate the ease that innovation brings to modern life. I love to be safe and warm in my house, watching my TV and using the internet, taking food from my fridge and sleeping in a comfortable bed. I'm truly grateful every day for these things that so many people take for granted and others will never experience. I'm just suggesting that we need to consider the impact of our choices on ourselves and the planet and make these decisions consciously.

Putting anything unnatural into your body, and then ultimately into the soil or waterways, but still expecting a natural result or outcome is crazy. Your DNA has been shaped by nature over millions of years to provide abundant health and perfect function. You are a perfectly organised ecosystem of 75 trillion cells, all working in perfect harmony, with the sole intention of creating health. But bombarding them with unnatural substances contained in your foods, in the multiple medications you're advised to take and in the polluted air you breathe can only result in a loss of health.

Choose more natural products whenever you can; they're probably better for you and for the planet. By this I mean toiletries, cleaning products and clothing. Buy organic whenever possible. I know it costs more in terms of the money you have to spend but don't think of it as expensive. Organic foods cost more to buy because they currently cost more to produce. I've never chosen organic fruits and vegetables because of a potentially higher nutrient density. If that were the reason, I may as well stick to industrially grown versions but just eat a little more to give me the extra vitamins! I choose organic to minimise my exposure to petroleum-based fertilisers and chemical pesticides. Chemical pesticides and fertilisers are a way of growing food cheaply and maximising profits for corporations, but at what cost? Polluting the planet and our bodies and reducing the health of both at the same time.

Organic vegetables and free-range, naturally reared meats cost what food should cost to produce. We've become so accustomed to ever cheaper prices from modern mass production that we've forgotten how much food *should* cost! A couple of generations ago, a large amount of an average family's monthly income was spent on putting food on the table and this was just accepted as the norm. Nowadays, we want that but also the latest mobile phone, subscription TV services, foreign holidays and all the other trappings of modern life, so food has become cheaper and cheaper, providing lower quality and less benefit to the consumer as a result.

If we all prioritised natural and organic products, the farmers and retailers would produce more and the prices would fall. There would be less toxic waste flushed down our toilets and poured into our drains, leading to our health and that of the planet improving. Surely we owe it to the thousands of generations of our ancestors who got us this far, and to the children of our children's children who are yet to come.

About the Author

Spencer Pullin was born and educated in Scunthorpe, Lincolnshire. He left school at 16 and, after completing an apprenticeship and a degree, spent 15 years in the steel industry as an electrician and electrical engineer.

After meeting his future wife Julia on a blind date, his life took a completely different direction, resulting in him leaving engineering behind and instead owning and managing The Chirohealth Clinic with her. During their 16 years of business ownership, he has been exposed to many leaders in the field of true health and wellbeing and has formed his own opinions based on logical thought and reasoning.

Spencer lives with Julia, their son Clarry and their four white ducks in Lincolnshire, UK.

Stay in Touch

www.naturalogy.co.uk

www.facebook.com/naturalogybook

Email Spencer at:

spencer@naturalogy.co.uk